Amy Bizzarri

111 Places for Kids in Chicago That You Must Not Miss

Photographs by Susie Inverso

D1564935

emons:

To Daniel and Chiara, with love. A.B.

*To Max and Vincent, my nephews who seem
to always be seeking adventure. We have a big list of places
to hit up next time you visit! S.I.*

MIX
Paper from
responsible sources
FSC® C043106

© Emons Verlag GmbH
All rights reserved
© Photographs by Susie Inverso, except: Ape Cognition Care Time (ch. 5):
Todd Rosenberg Photography; Blue Island Brewmasters (ch. 13): Joyce Sheldon;
Children's Afternoon Tea (ch. 19): Pavilion at The Langham,Chicago; Method
Soap Factory (ch. 65): method; Midnight Circus (ch. 66): Sharon Gaietto;
Night at the Museum, Aquarium, or Zoo (ch. 73): Museum of Science
and Industry, Chicago; Perry Mastodon (ch. 80): Wheaton College; Surf Lake
Michigan (ch. 95): Michelle Nozykowski; Thorne Miniature Rooms (ch. 101):
The Art Institute of Chicago; Windy City Rollers (ch 108): Steve Jurkovic;
Willowbrook Wildlife Center (ch. 107): Willowbrook Wildlife Center
© Cover motif: shutterstock.com/Dan Thornberg; Tupungato;
Konstantin L; Maria Burmistrova; Vereshchagin Dmitry; Joe Hendrickson
Edited by Karen E. Seiger
Layout: Editorial Design & Artdirection, Conny Laue, Bochum,
based on a design by Lübbeke | Naumann | Thoben and Nina Schäfer
Maps: altancicek.design, www.altancicek.de
Basic cartographical information from Openstreetmap,
© OpenStreetMap-Mitwirkende, ODbL
Printing and binding: Grafisches Centrum Cuno, Calbe
Printed in Germany 2019
ISBN 978-3-7408-0599-9
First edition

Did you enjoy this guidebook? Would you like to see more?
Join us in uncovering new places around the world at:
www.111places.com

FOREWORD

Can you imagine a wonderland where you can...

Visit a mermaid who washed up on the shores of Lake Michigan? Play with a ghost in a graveyard? Kiss a beluga whale?

Well, guess what? You can have all of these amazing experiences right here in Chicago!

Have you ever chatted with (animatronic) former Mayor Harold Washington? Sat in on a gorilla cognitive therapy session? Hand fed a kale salad to a giraffe? Walked a labyrinth? Cheered on a baseball game... that plays according to the rules of 1800? Have you ever floated under fireworks? Stepped inside a Chicago-style movable bridge? Zoomed up above the skyscrapers in a helicopter?

This guidebook is your chance to explore our great city with your favorite kids in tow.

I've carefully honed a bucket list of 111 fascinating experiences that will engage curious kids of all ages, including those of you who are kids at heart.

As I researched this book, I came across several staggering statistics. Kids today spend an average of six hours per day staring at electronic devices. Parents spend more than nine hours a day with their faces directed towards a screen. Meanwhile, the American Academy of Pediatrics warns that overuse of digital media and screens can put children and teens at risk of obesity, sleep problems, cyberbullying, and underperforming at school.

Childhood is fleeting. The days are long but the years are short, so the saying goes. In the blink of an eye, your kids will be heading off into this great big world on adventures of their very own.

This book is my invitation to kids and parents to get off the screens and into the great outdoors, where the history and culture of our great city, as well as fun adventures galore, are just waiting to be discovered.

A.B.

111 PLACES

1_AJI ICHIBAN

Munchies paradise

Aji Ichiban transforms the typical penny-candy shop visit. Yes, you still take a small, white bag and examine the colorful rows of candy-filled bins for your favorites before heading to the register to have your loot weighed. But the favorites here are decidedly different.

Grab your passport – your taste buds are about to embark on a sweet adventure. At this, the US flagship for one of the largest snack companies in Hong Kong, candies of all shapes, sizes, colors, and flavors – salty and sweet – fill the shelves and the bins to the brim.

Forget boring old chocolate or caramel and give kumquat pellets, dried cuttlefish, super-salted plums, crispy baby crabs, or tomato gummies a try. Shredded squid and shrimp crisps are other popular picks. Even the American brands featured here take on altogether new and interesting flavors: KitKats are filled with layers of pureed sweet potatoes; Oreos trade their vanilla cream filling with matcha; Lay's Potato Chips arrive sprinkled with Kyushu seaweed. Be sure to taste the lychee-flavored hard candy, the kiwi chewing gum, and the Botan Rice Candy (its wrapper melts in your mouth!).

Aji Ichiban is a great place to encourage your child to expand their palate. Small bowls of samples give you a chance to try before you buy, so kids (and adults) will more than likely find a unique, new favorite. Kids with adventuresome tastebuds will want to give the Isoyaki Duck Gizzards a try, or crunch into the Kanikko Tiny Japanese Crabs, which are salty, sweet, and crispy whole baby crabs.

yes

TIP: Are you a snake? A ram? A rabbit? Head to the courtyard at the center of China Place to find the Chinese zodiac animal that corresponds to your birth year.

Address 2117 S. China Place, Chicago, IL 60616, +1 (312) 328-9998, www.ajiichiban.com.hk/eng/index.php, info@ajiichiban.com.hk // Getting there Red Line to Cermak–Chinatown // Hours Daily 11am–8pm // Ages 3+

2__AMERICAN SCIENCE & SURPLUS

Gadgets, gizmos, whosits, and whatsits galore

Have you been searching high and low for extra-long cotton swabs, sized to clean an elephant's ears? Hoping to secure a life-size bat skeleton ASAP? Planning on building your very own robot this weekend and need all the requisite gadgets and gizmos? You'll find everything you didn't know you needed at American Science & Surplus, *the* store for curious, STEM-minded kids.

Though it's been serving the scientific community for over 75 years thanks to its unbeatable selection of stuff – weird, wacky, multipurpose, or unknown purpose stuff – the supply here goes beyond lab standards. Rubber chickens share space with glass beakers; a portable, two-person military latrine is posed next to a giant weather balloon. Plan to spend at least an hour digging through these goodies. A word of caution: when a surplus item is gone, it is gone for good. So if you see something that piques your curiosity, buy it today because it likely won't be available tomorrow.

Founder Al Luebbers was working for Western Electric when he noticed that a company next door to the plant where he worked was throwing away reject lenses. He asked them if he could buy the rejects, and they said, "No, but you can have them if you will haul them away." Realizing he could resell odds and ends for a profit, he opened American Science & Surplus in the late 1930s. To this day, closeouts, inventory overruns, mis-manufactures, and items whose time has not come find their way to the shelves at this browse-worthy store.

Address 5316 N. Milwaukee Avenue, Chicago, IL 60630, +1 (773) 763-0313, www.sciplus.com, info@sciplus.com // Getting there Blue Line to Jefferson Park, or Metra UP-NW to Gladstone Park // Hours Mon–Wed & Fri 10am–7pm, Thu 10am–8pm, Sat 10am–6pm, Sun 11am–5pm // Ages 3+

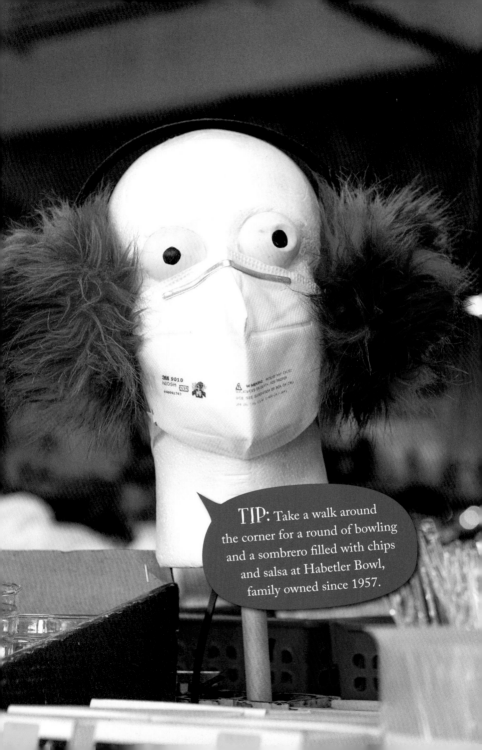

TIP: Take a walk around the corner for a round of bowling and a sombrero filled with chips and salsa at Habetler Bowl, family owned since 1957.

3_ ANCIENT EGYPTIAN TEMPLE

Move like an Egyptian

On November 4, 1922, British archaeologist Howard Carter discovered a step leading to a hidden tomb in the Valley of the Kings in Egypt. Later that month, he descended into the four-room chamber to discover the amazingly intact tomb of King Tutankhamun. The so-called Boy King was entombed in three nested coffins within a stone sarcophagus. The final coffin, which held the mummified body of King Tut safe for more than 3,000 years, was made of brilliant, solid gold.

Carter's discovery set off Egyptomania, a renewed interest in all things ancient Egypt.

Around that same time in Chicago, the Reebie Storage and Moving Co., owned by brothers John and William Reebie, was planning to construct a new building for their business. The brothers, inspired by Egyptian Revival architecture, decided to create an ancient Egyptian temple of their very own, smack dab in the middle of the North Side neighborhood of Lincoln Park. Fittingly, the moving and storage company's logo became a pharaonic sphinx head. As Arthur Reebie, William's son, noted, "The Egyptians were the first moving and storage men. They floated the grain down the Nile and stored it for use during the lean times or famine."

The building's design was based on two ancient Egyptian temples, Dendera and Edfu, erected about 200 B.C. by Pharaoh Ramses II. Note the two statues of Ramses, representative of the two founding Reebie brothers, that flank the entrance. See how many winged scarabs, or dung beetles, you can find on the façade.

Address 2325 N. Clark Street, Chicago, IL 60614, www.reebieallied.com // Getting there Brown, Purple, or Red Line to Fullerton // Hours Unrestricted from the outside only // Ages 3+

TIP: Try and test your hieroglyph reading skills too. From right to left, the hieroglyphs on the façade read, "I have put protection upon your furniture and all sealed things. I have guarded all your property every day warding off devouring flames and likewise robbery."

REEBIE

4_ ANTIQUE ELEVATOR RIDE

Chicago's oldest lifts at the Fine Arts Building

Step inside the elevators at the Fine Arts Building, and you'll immediately notice two oddities: the lack of buttons and the human operator.

The three elegant elevators are the oldest in the city, original to the building, which opened in 1885 as a factory and showroom for Studebaker carriages. Three elevators stop at each of the building's 10 floors, offering the opportunity to experience how the vertical transportation device functioned before technology made the experience altogether swifter and seamless. The whirr of the engines, the clinking of the chains, and the many jolts, jerks, squeaks, and thuds make this elevator experience a mild version of the ominous ride *Tower of Terror*, at Walt Disney World.

You'll have to wait in view of the glass windows so the operator can spot you and stop to pick you up in the first place. Then you'll have to let the operator know your destination.

In 1898, the building was converted to studio and gallery spaces, and students of the fine and performing arts have been boarding the elevators to make their way to voice classes, dance rehearsals, instrument tunings, and general inspiration for over a century.

The inscription that greets visitors passing through the entrance hall is a potent reminder of the artistic passions that have been cultivated here: All Passes – Art Alone Endures.

Address 410 S. Michigan Avenue, Chicago, IL 60605, +1 (312) 566-9800, www.fineartsbuilding.com, info@fineartsbuilding.com // Getting there Brown, Orange, Pink, or Purple Line to Harold Washington Library-State/Van Buren // Hours Mon–Fri 7am–10pm, Sat 7am–9pm, Sun 9am–9pm // Ages 3+

TIP: On the second Friday of every month, the Fine Arts Building hosts an open house. Roam the floors and meet the artists, free of charge, from 5 to 9pm.

5_ APE COGNITION CARE TIME

Understanding our closest cousins

Spend some time with the chimpanzees and gorillas of the Regenstein Center for African Apes at the Lincoln Park Zoo, and you're bound to notice some surprising similarities with humans. Just like us, they live in small groups, or 'troops,' which we humans call families. Some apes have been observed using tools in the wild. Many have even learned to use sign language to communicate with humans. As our closest living relatives in the animal kingdom, apes can help us better understand ourselves.

Every day at 1:30pm, the zoologists carve out some time to study how apes think and learn. Visitors are invited to watch the thinking games go down. Watch as the gorillas and chimps solve puzzles on touchscreen computers, use tools to earn food rewards, and learn how to participate in their own health care. The apes in return benefit by honing their cognition skills.

At 29,000 square feet, the $26-million center is the most expensive building ever constructed at the zoo. The space is divided into three areas: the Kovler Gorilla Bamboo Forest, the Strangler Fig Forest, and the Dry Riverbed Valley. The gorillas and chimpanzees who live there can usually be found sitting on the bamboo stands, swinging from the trees and 5,000 feet of artificial vines, or sitting outdoors on the logs (they're heated!).

See if you can spot the tiniest members of the western lowland gorilla family. Born in May and June, 2019, two babies were born into a troop of seven adults, including adult females Bana and Bahati, and three juvenile females: Bella, Nayembi, and Patty.

TIP: Kids can make like an ape at the Treetop Canopy Climbing Adventure, located inside the Pritzker Family Children's Zoo main building.

Address Regenstein Center for African Apes, Lincoln Park Zoo, 2001 N. Clark Street, Chicago, IL 60614, +1 (312) 742-2000, www.lpzoo.org // Getting there CTA bus 151 or 156 to Stockton & Armitage // Hours Daily at 1:30pm // Ages 3+

6_AQUAMERMAID

Mermaid training academy for landlubbers

Have you ever dreamed of trading your feet... for fins?

If you're a wannabe mermaid, ordinary schools just aren't going to make the cut when it comes to learning the ways of the merfolk. Thankfully, there is one school in Chicago that features student uniforms with scales, a focus on seashell identification smarts over reading, writing, and arithmetic, and teachers who give Ariel a run for her marine money. Chicago's very own AquaMermaid is a place where kids (and kids at heart!) can learn all the maritime life skills they'll ever need to know, from fin high fives to deep treasure dives. Instructors will have you guiding ships into safe harbors and waving your fins to passing sailors in no time. You'll learn the 'sailor wave' in class.

AquaMermaid provides you with an amazing monofin and a snazzy spandex mermaid tail. Your special monofin will make it easier and speedier than ever to glide through the water. Classes here are arranged by both swimming level and age. You'll have to be at least seven years old, however, and comfortable enough swimming with a spandex tail and a fin on your feet, to set off on an AquaMermaid adventure. But some exceptions can be made, so talk to your Aqua-Mermaid registrar before you head to the high seas (pool) of the UIC Sports and Fitness Center.

Kids get to choose the color fin that best fits their aquatic personality. You'll feel so glam in your mermaid gear that you'll want to capture the look on camera. Thankfully, the last 10 minutes of class are reserved for photo opps. Even better, outfit your smartphone with a waterproof case so you can document all the underwater action yourself.

Address Small Pool, UIC, 901 W. Roosevelt Road, Chicago, IL 60608, +1 (866 279-2767, www.aquamermaid.com/collections/chicago, chicago@aquamermaid.com // Getting there Blue Line to UIC/Halsted // Hours See website for schedule // Ages 5+

TIP: Give your bathtub a bubbly, glitzy, mermaid-friendly vibe with a glittery bath bomb from Distinct Bath and Body. Owner and soap artisan Sam makes each batch by hand in the in-store studio using natural and locally sourced, plant-based ingredients and oils.

7_BAJIISHKA'OGAAN LODGE

Keepers of the fire

Gneshnabem ne? Do you speak Bodewadmimwen?

If you could step back in time and explore 18th-century Chicagoland, you'd likely hear Bodewadmimwen, the language of the Potawatomi Nation.

The Potawatomi – who call themselves Bodéwadmi, or 'keepers of the fire' – migrated to the Chicago region from what's now Niagara Falls in the late 1600s, settling along the Calumet, Chicago, and Des Plaines Rivers. Andrew Jackson's Indian Removal Act of 1830, followed by the Chicago Treaty of 1833, ultimately removed thousands of Potawatomi from their homes and forced them onto the 'Trail of Death,' from the Great Lakes region to reservations beyond the Mississippi in Missouri, Iowa, and Kansas.

At Evanston's Mitchell Museum of the American Indian, kids can settle into a *Bajiishka'ogaan*, a low-lying, conical lodge typically built by the Potawatomi for hunting and fishing expeditions. Take a seat on a grass mat, close the deer-hide door, and warm up by the (fake) fire at its center. The entire lodge is surrounded by a mural depicting the landscape and ecosystem in Chicago, Evanston, and Skokie, highlighting the plants and animals that would have been part of the lives of the Potawatomi.

On Saturdays from 11am to noon and Sundays 12:30 to 1:30pm, kids are invited to make simple versions of traditional Native American items that once would have been found in a lodge such as this, including talking feathers, button blankets, and quill boxes.

Address 3001 Central Street, Evanston, IL 60201, +1 (847) 475-1030, www.mitchellmuseum.org // Getting there Metra UP-N to Central Street Evanston // Hours Tue–Sat 10am–5pm, Sun noon–4pm // Ages 5+

TIP: Hartigan's Ice Cream, an old-fashioned, neighborhood ice cream parlor. Screenwriter Moira McMahon worked here in the early 1990s – spot Hartigan's in her Netflix hit *A Light Beneath Their Feet*.

8_BAPS SHRI SWAMI-NARAYAN MANDIR

Timeless temple

In the Chicago suburb of Bartlett, a breathtaking *mandir*, a traditional Hindu place of worship, captures the sunrises and sunsets with its inspiring architecture. Located on a complex of over 27 acres, the mandir, the largest of its kind in Illinois, was built according to guidelines outlined in the *Shilpa Shastras*, ancient Hindu architectural texts. Wander the elegantly landscaped grounds with the glorious temple as a backdrop, and you're bound to feel transported to India, if not the heavens.

Perhaps the secret to the mandir's majesty lies in its limestone and marble stones. Quarried from Turkey and Italy, 70,000 cubic feet of stone was shipped to Rajasthan, where it was hewn and carved into intricate patterns by 2,000 craftsmen. Then all 40,000 pieces of stone set off on the long voyage to Chicago. Once they arrived, they were fitted together like a jigsaw puzzle into the 78-feet-high x 112-feet-wide x 215-feet-long mandir complete with 151 pillars, 117 arches, five pinnacles, and four balconies, and feted with a 16-day celebration.

Within the mandir, a series of shrines feature sacred images of Hindu deities. *Swaminarayan sadhus* (Hindu monks) offer devotional worship to these deities throughout the day, beginning before dawn with morning hymns. In the evening, food is offered to the murtis, and they are put to rest with night garments.

Below the mandir, the exhibit *Understanding Hinduism* introduces visitors to the history and beliefs behind Hinduism. Encourage your kids to ask questions to the staff, who will happily share their faith.

TIP: Head on over to nearby Jaynesway Farm for a pony ride! A parent or adult leads the pony around the path and a 30-minute ride is $15.00.

Address 1851 Pramukh Swami Road,
Bartlett, IL 60103, +1 (630) 213-2277,
www.baps.org/Global-Network/
North-America/Chicago.aspx //
Getting there Take I-90/94 west
(towards O'Hare Airport), keep on
I-90 west towards Rockford for
25 miles, take Route 59 exit, and travel
south on Route 59 for 8 miles //
Hours Daily 9am–7:30pm // Ages 5+

9_BARREL OF MONKEYS

That's weird, Grandma

Barrel of Monkeys (BOM) brings stories to life... literally.

It's where teaching artists find inspiration in the fabulous stories that are told by the many kids that attend Chicago Public Schools (CPS) around the city.

Now in its eighteenth year, BOM's ongoing, weekly sketch show features adaptations of stories written during their creative writing residencies hosted at local elementary schools. The stories then jump from page to stage with a little help from BOM's incredible team of professional actors, comedians, and musicians, who work one-on-one with students to write (usually off-the-wall) stories that are then translated to stage-worthy sketches. The result: *That's Weird, Grandma*, a.k.a. the most original sketch comedy revue in the city that brought you *Second City*, hosted every Sunday at 3pm.

Prepare to laugh; prepare to cry. The stories that these 3rd–5th graders dream up are almost always outrageous. Every week, the BOM team weaves them into an entirely new line-up of stories, dialogs, and musical numbers. BOM invites audiences to vote for their favorites at each performance, making it an ever-changing, standing Sunday date to keep.

The show is hosted at the Neo-Futurarium, a former dance hall, Romanian library, and community center converted into one of the most eclectic and memorable theater spaces in Chicago. Check out the portraits of US presidents, painted by local CPS students, that line the entrance hallway.

Address 5153 N. Ashland Avenue, Chicago, IL 60640,
+1 (773) 506-7140, www.barrelofmonkeys.org // Getting there
Red Line to Berwyn // Hours Sun 3–4:05pm // Ages 6+

TIP: Introduce your kids to the powerful force that is sketch improv at Second City's Youth & Teen Ensemble, a fifty-minute show consisting of improv and sketch on Saturdays at 6pm.

10_ BELMONT FEED AND SEED

The birds and the bees need to eat too

Dogs and cats make for wonderful pets... but have you considered opening your home to a homing pigeon? Why not welcome a brood of chicks into your backyard? How about a swarm of bumblebees?

Even if you're not quite ready to establish your very own backyard menagerie, Belmont Feed and Seed, Chicago's specialty store for people who keep pigeons, bees, chickens, and other poultry in an urban setting, is a fantastic place to indulge your hidden farming fantasies. The chickens that stroll the aisles and cluck from their cages are smart, sassy, and adorable. Look for the silkies standing ready to strut the runway thanks to their fancy, feathery-topped caps. The homing pigeons here proudly declare their utter genius. Did you know that they possess a group of neurons that process the polarity of the Earth's magnetic fields? That's how they can be trained to deliver messages and always find their way back to their home sweet home. The store also carries live working hives and bees, in case you're considering setting up your own honey-making operation.

Owners Dan and Lidia Andronic are always on hand at their zoo of a store to answer any pressing questions, while their terrier Mickey keeps the birds and human customers in check. "Chickens and pigeons make for wonderful companions," underscores Dan. "The chickens especially will follow you around like little, playful puppets. And nothing beats gathering fresh eggs from your backyard farm."

Address 3036 W. Belmont Avenue, Chicago, IL 60618, +1 (773) 588-1144, www.belmontfeedandseed.com // Getting there Blue Line to Belmont // Hours Tue–Fri 10am–6pm, Sat 10am–4pm, Sun 11am–3pm // Ages 3+

11_BELUGA ENCOUNTER
Meet and greet with a sweet white whale

Dreaming of dancing with a beluga whale? Or perhaps your wish upon a star is just one small kiss on the cheek from a lovable cetacean?

Don't think you'll need to catch the next flight to the Arctic Circle. Instead, count on the Shedd Aquarium to grant your whale-sized dreams and set you up with a melonhead, a.k.a. *Delphinapterus leucas*.

The Shedd Aquarium's Beluga Encounter experience is a gift that no ocean-loving kid will soon forget. The incredible program gives kids the exclusive chance to go behind the scenes at this world-class aquarium, home to 32,600 marine animals, from snails to whales, and literally dip their landlubbing legs into the Abbott Oceanarium's three-million-gallon tank that is the home of eight charming belugas.

Your beluga encounter begins with an informative orientation about training and animal care. Then you'll pull on waders to enter the Grainger Beluga Encounter Habitat, where, standing side by side with a trainer on an underwater ledge, you'll come face to face with a white whale. You'll touch the beluga's skin and try a few training techniques, and you will learn why these incredible creatures are nicknamed the 'canaries of the sea.'

Beluga Encounter tickets also include express entry to the aquarium, admission to all exhibits, and a ticket to the next available aquatic presentation. Participants must be at least 60 inches tall and children up to 15 years old must be accompanied by a participating adult age 18 or older, also with a paid ticket.

TIP: Before you leave the aquarium, go find *Man with Fish*, an unusual, 16-foot sculpture of a man embracing a fish, created by German artist Stephan Balkenhol.

Address Shedd Aquarium, 1200 S. Lake Shore Drive, Chicago, IL 60605, +1 (312) 939-2438, www.sheddaquarium.org // Getting there Green, Orange, or Red Line to Roosevelt // Hours See website for seasonal hours //Ages 5+

12_BIKE THE DRIVE

Lake Shore Drive on two wheels

A drive along Chicago's Lake Shore Drive, with the city skyline on one side of you and sparkling Lake Michigan on the other, is sublime. Year round, you can bike the 19-mile-long Lakefront Trail, which extends from Ardmore Street (5800 N. Sheridan Road) on the North Side to 71st Street (7100 S. South Shore Drive) on the South Side. Take away the traffic, though, and it's a slice of heaven.

One summertime Sunday per year, usually late May, Lake Shore Drive is closed to cars, turning one of the most fantastic expressways in the world into an unforgettable biking experience. Bike the Drive isn't a competition but rather a chance to ride along this normally trafficked highway and enjoy the scenery along the way. Even kids are invited to hop into their bike seats or onto their very own bikes and pedal away along LSD in this annual ride.

You'll have to register for this event, but take heart: all proceeds from Bike the Drive support the Active Transportation Alliance, a coalition of people working to make biking, walking, and transit safe and easy options for every city citizen.

The entire Bike the Drive loop is 30 super scenic miles, but you can make your ride as short or long as you like by using turnarounds located along the route. Three rest stops offer riders light snacks, fruit, and water. Bring your own water bottle to cut down on waste. And plan on arriving early: the event begins at 5:30am, but you can start at 7am at the latest to get the most out of your ride.

TIP: Take your bike on trains and buses operated by CTA, Metra, and Pace. The CTA relaxes their two bikes per car policy for Bike the Drive. Or rent a bike at Bike and Roll Chicago.

Address Lakefront Trail between Ardmore Avenue and 71st Street, Chicago, see www.bikethedrive.org for routes // Getting there Multiple entry points for Lakefront Trail; see website // Hours Lakefront Trail: dawn–dusk; Bike the Drive: 5:30–10:15am // Ages 3+

13_BLUE ISLAND BREWMASTERS VINTAGE BASE BALL CLUB

Take me out to the old ball game

Baseball was a whole lot different in the 1800s, when pitchers were called 'hurlers', catchers 'the behind', and the fans 'cranks.' A walk was six balls, not four. When a foul ball was caught after the first bounce, a.k.a. a 'bamboozle,' the batter was out. Hurlers threw underhand, and nobody used gloves. It was a gentlemanly game; spitting, stealing bases, swearing, and sliding into home base were strictly forbidden.

The Brewmasters play base ball (as it was originally, two words) according to the rules of 1858. Their home field is the Gas Works Grounds on the corner of James and Ann Streets in Blue Island, about 15 miles from the Chicago Loop and one of the largest settlements in the southern part of Cook County. The area was an important center of commerce and culture in the middle of the nineteenth century.

This is one of the most charming games to catch in action. The players wear old-fashioned uniforms, often with suspenders, and they always play for fun with other regional vintage baseball teams, though competition can be heated. Brewmasters' practices are open to the public and held each Thursday (weather permitting) at 6:30pm. Ask your baseball-playing kids if they can spot the key differences between vintage and modern-day baseball. Bring a blanket or folding chairs and get ready to reconnect with the true spirit of the game.

> TIP: Check out *Baseball: Then to WOW!* from your local library. Written by the editors of Sports Illustrated Kids, this guide to all things baseball shows readers how the sport evolved from the early days to today.

Address Gas Works Grounds at the intersection of James and Ann Streets, Blue Island, IL 60406, www.blueislandhistoricalsociety.com/blue-island-brewmasters-vintage-base-ball // Getting there Metra RI to Blue Island Vermont Street // Hours See website for schedule // Ages 3+

14_BRUNK CHILDREN'S MUSEUM OF IMMIGRATION

In search of a better tomorrow

Imagine saying goodbye to the only life you've known, sailing away in steerage on a steamship, and stepping foot onto a new, promised land, where a new language, culture, and plenty of hard work await you and your family. The Brunk Children's Museum of Immigration bridges the past and the present, giving children a small taste of the challenging lives of the immigrants who built Chicago.

Kids at this hands-on-only museum will enter Old World Sweden first to see a traditional Scandinavian red stuga house and experience a variety of farm chores. Then it's time to make the trip to the New World via a replica 20-foot steam ship. Upon arrival in America, kids can settle into a pioneer log cabin and get to work milking the cow, farming a small plot of land, setting the table for dinner, and bringing in firewood.

Once upon a time, there were more Swedes in Chicago than in any city outside of Stockholm. In the late 1800s, the Swedish-born population in Chicago increased by roughly 233 percent, and by 1930, there were 65,735 Swedish-born Chicagoans. Most settled here in the North Side neighborhood of Andersonville, where you'll find the Brunk Children's Museum of Immigration housed within the Swedish American Museum.

Try to plan your visit for the third Friday of the month, when the museum hosts *Hejsan!* (Swedish for 'Hello!'), a themed story and craft hour focused on the museum's current exhibitions.

Address 5211 N. Clark Street, Chicago, IL 60640, +1 (773) 728-811, www.swedishamericanmuseum.org // **Getting there** Red Line to Berwyn // **Hours** Mon–Fri 10am–4pm, Sat & Sun 11am–4pm // **Ages** 3+

15_ CERNAN SPACE CENTER

Cosmic love across Earth and space

A trip to the moon is oh so complicated to plan, and the rocket ride there is oh so motion sickness inducing. Thankfully, the Cernan Earth and Space Center, a smaller-scale planetarium concealed on the campus of Triton College in River Grove, brings the stars to you via thrilling, space-science-focused laser projections on its magnificent, 44-foot-diameter Dome Theater.

Named for astronaut Eugene A. Cernan, who was born and raised in nearby Bellwood and a key member of the Gemini 9, Apollo 10, and Apollo 17 missions, the Cernan Earth and Space Center shares the same starry goal as the last astronaut to leave his footprints on the lunar surface: to inspire dreams and goals for a new generation of astronauts and explorers of all kinds.

While the educational, digital projections on the grand, 93-seat dome are the stars of this space center, stick around for a Cosmic Light Show, a trippy, unscientific, yet colorful laser extravaganza set to the tune of hippie faves like Pink Floyd, Mannheim Steamroller, and Jimi Hendrix.

One Saturday night each month, the Cernan Center offers its Skywatch program, which explores recent discoveries in the fields of astronomy and geoscience through fun activities and lively discussion. Don't forget to check out the on-site exhibits, too, which include Cernan's Apollo 10 space suit and, oddly, a full-scale model of a footprint and lower leg bone of a Brachiosaurus.

> TIP: Check out the unusual fossil exhibit, which displays a variety of Illinois fossils including our state fossil, the 'Tully Monster,' a soft-bodied bilaterian that lived in Illinois about 300 million years ago when the area was decidedly more tropical.

Address 2000 5th Avenue,
River Grove, IL 60171,
+1 (708) 583-3100,
www.triton.edu/cernan //
Getting there Blue Line to
Cumberland, then CTA bus
331 to 5th/Hemingway
Drive // **Hours** See website
or call for hours and
showtimes // **Ages** 3+

16_ CHICAGO FROM A HELICOPTER

Up, up, and away!

Planes, trains, automobiles... and helicopters? If there's a best way to see the city of Chicago in all its skyscraping glory, it's from the comfort of a high-flying helicopter. Buckle up and get ready to (gently) zoom 1,200 feet into the sky. Chicago Helicopter Experience invites families with kids as young as three years old to soar into the clouds on an unforgettable, whirlybird of an adventure.

The excitement begins at the heliport, conveniently located in Bridgeport. Before departing up above the city, you'll need to complete pre-flight training, which includes a general safety overview. While you're waiting for your six-seater 'copter to be prepped for departure, spend some time on the flight simulator to see if you have what it takes to pilot a chopper.

Your names are called, and you'll be whisked to a helicopter, stopping briefly for a fun photo opp. Your professional pilot will take you far above the skyline, where you'll spend about 15 minutes in the air. Noise-canceling headphones with a headset both protect little ears and also let you ask the pilot any questions as you enjoy the 25-mile ride past downtown and along the lakefront.

For an over-the-top helicopter experience, book a Fireworks Tour, and you'll be up in the sky, ready to capture the colorful Navy Pier fireworks that blast off on Wednesday and Saturday evenings at dusk throughout the summer, from Memorial Day through Labor Day. Or see Chicago all dressed up for the holidays from the cozy comfort of a luxury helicopter on a CHE Holiday Lights Experience tour, offered on select days the week before Thanksgiving through December 31.

Address CHE Chicago Heliport, 2420 S. Halsted Street, Chicago, IL 60608, +1 (312) 967-8687, www.chicagohelicopterexperience.com, info@chetours.com // **Getting there** Orange Line to Halsted // **Hours** See website for tours // **Ages** 3+

TIP: For flights a little closer to the ground, visit the Schiller Model Airplane Flying Field.

17 _ CHICAGO MAGIC LOUNGE

Abracadabra!

From the late 1800s to the Roaring Twenties, Chicago brimmed with magicians. Most came to the rapidly growing city to make their magic mark at the 1893 World's Colombian Exposition and then stayed to perform their acts in Vaudeville theaters, neighborhood shops, taverns, and even on street corners.

Chicago Magic Lounge brings back the golden era of magic with an entertaining show in a top-secret venue.

5050 North Clark Street only *looks* like your typical laundromat. But step inside, ring the bell, and a trick door, concealed behind retro washing machines, will swing open – a big surprise for unsuspecting kids. From the laundromat, you'll be transported into a small, charming library filled with magic books and memorabilia, including a magazine cover signed by none other than Harry Houdini himself. Then yet another trick door – a bookshelf – will slowly open to reveal the intimate, Art Deco-inspired cabaret theater.

Patrons of the performance bar must be 21, but every Sunday the Magic Lounge offers daytime shows suitable for ages 5 and up, giving little ones the chance to experience close-up, old-school tableside magic in a speakeasy-like setting. Coins will disappear and reappear behind ears, paper snakes will pop out of hats, and an endless rainbow of scarves will unfurl before your very eyes. While you're witnessing all the magic, dig into a menu of kid-sized bites accompanied by kiddie cocktails. The 45-minute show is highly interactive, and kids are periodically asked to wave their invisible wands or assist onstage to help out with a trick or two.

Address 5050 N. Clark Street, Chicago, IL 60640, +1 (312) 366-4500, www.chicagomagiclounge.com, info@chicagomagiclounge.com // Getting there Red Line to Argyle // Hours Sun noon, reservations required // Ages 5+

18_ CHICAGO RIVER BRIDGE LIFTS

Look inside an engineering marvel

It's no surprise that Chicago is considered the movable bridge capital of the world. Our city's so-called bascule bridges accommodate cars, trucks, bicycles, trains, pedestrians – everything and anyone wishing to cross the river. In a matter of eight minutes, the bridges lift and lower, giving safe passage to the many barges and boats making their way from the river to the lake and back. When all 20 of the downtown drawbridges open at once, it's a magical act of synchronicity and a marvel of engineering combined into one do-not-miss experience.

Part of the double-decker Michigan Avenue (now DuSable) bridge is the McCormick Bridgehouse and Chicago River Museum, which gives visitors the chance to step inside an iconic movable bridge. Watch firsthand as all the large and small gears work in sync to raise the massive span of steel. Located on the south end of Michigan Avenue, the museum begins at river level and spirals five stories up. Friends of the Chicago River opened the unique museum in 2006 "to provide new access and understanding of the dynamic relationship between Chicago and its river." The museum also welcomes fishy friends: Chicago's one and only fish hotel is located in the river, beside the bridgehouse, providing a safe harbor for the many sunfish, bluegills, and carp that call the river home.

The museum's educational exhibits showcase the history of both the river and the science behind the spectacle, all of which is fascinating any time of year. But check the museum's schedule and try to time your visit to coincide with one of the 40+ planned synchronized bridge lifts that take place April through November.

Address 99 Chicago Riverwalk, Chicago, IL 60611, +1 (312) 977-0227, www.bridgehousemuseum.org // Getting there Brown, Orange, Purple, Green, or Pink Line to Clark/Lake // Hours May–Oct, daily 10am–5pm // Ages 3+

TIP: A bust of black pioneer and entrepreneur Jean Baptiste Point Du Sable, the first permanent, non-Indigenous settler of what would later become Chicago, marks the riverside location where, around the 1780s, he built his trading post and lived with wife Kitihawa and children.

19_ CHILDREN'S AFTERNOON TEA

Feelin' fancy at the Langham Hotel

Long catering to royals, London's Langham Hotel stands as the city's grandest, most gilded hotel of all. When it opened on Regent Street in 1865, it was the first European hotel to serve afternoon tea, introducing the indulgent ritual, perfect for warding off tummy growls between lunch and dinner, at a cost of one shilling and sixpence.

Chicago's five-star Langham Hotel is just as elegant, housed in a mid-century modern skyscraper, the last work of acclaimed architect Mies van der Rohe.

Every afternoon, connoisseurs of lingering over a cup of tea and dainty bites descend on the airy, art-filled tea room, where unparalleled service and presentation offer the best afternoon tea in the city. Children are always welcome, with a special menu made just for them, because it's never too early to teach your kids the fine art of feelin' fancy. They'll love stirring in a sugar cube or two and sipping their own herbal tea blend, a specially sourced herbal infusion with notes of dried rooibos, flowers, and rhubarb, accompanied by dozens of finger-sized, savory and sweet delights that are served on tiered platters. It's a great excuse to don your dressy duds.

During the dreary winter months of January and February, the tea is Alice in Wonderland themed. The cookies arrive shaped like a deck of cards, the scones sprinkled with rainbow confetti, and the finger sandwiches striped like an elusive Cheshire cat.

Afternoon tea at the Langham is a once-upon-a time treat for all Mad-Hatters.

> **TIP:** If you love the sparkling glass bubbles that dangle above your heads, pay a visit to yet another of Anish Kapoor's baubles, Millennium Park's Cloud Gate, a.k.a. 'The Bean.'

Address 330 N. Wabash Avenue, Chicago, IL 60611, +1 (773) 923-9988, www.langhamhotels.com/chicago, tlchi.info@langhamhotels.com // **Getting there** Red Line to Grand/State // **Hours** Mon–Fri 3–5pm, Sat & Sun 1–5pm // **Ages 3+**

20 _ COSMIC BOWL

Bowl and glow at Waveland Bowl

Waveland Bowl is the largest bowling alley in Chicago. Forty lanes, all with automatic scoring, are usually packed with bowlers ready to score a strike. Eight times each week, the lights go dark, the black lights glow, multicolor lights disco dance around the entire alley, dance music blasts from surround speakers, and a fog machine blows, adding an entirely otherworldly element to your everyday bowling match. If you've ever dreamed of bowling on another planet, head to Waveland Bowl for Cosmic Bowl.

How do black, a.k.a. ultraviolet, lights work? Though it appears dark purple, most of the light that black light emits is in the ultraviolet (UV) range of the spectrum, which is invisible to the human eye.

Under UV light, white clothes (and white teeth!) glow in the dark, and fluorescent colored clothes emit a bright, colorful glow. That's because they contain phosphors, any substance that absorbs energy and re-emits it as visible light. Under black light, phosphors convert the UV radiation they receive into visible light.

Waveland Bowl welcomes even the tiniest of bowlers by giving them the chance to hit a pin or two thanks to lane bumpers that make gutter balls a thing of the past – just be sure to ask for the bumpers to be raised upon check-in. A billiards area, a children's movie theater, a fast food restaurant (and two bars for Mom and Dad) make this the ultimate place to have a little bit of family fun. Bowl on a day when Cosmic Bowl is in full swing for even more out-of-this-world fun.

> TIP: Waveland Bowl participates in the Kids Bowl Free All Summer Long program. Register kids at www.kidsbowlfree.com and receive two free games per day all summer long.

Address 3700 N. Western Avenue, Chicago, IL 60618, +1 (773) 472-5900, www.wavelandbowl.com // Getting there Brown Line to Addison; Blue Line to Western, then CTA bus 49 to Western & Addison // Hours See website for Cosmic Bowl hours // Ages 3+

21_ COWS ON PARADE

Remaining free-range bovines of Chi-cow-go

Cows often met their brutal end in Chicago. At its peak, the 475-acre Union Stockyards slaughtered a whopping 18 million animals a year. But in the summer of 1999, a herd of cows ambled into town and was invited to stay for a spell. These weren't just any old cows. These were the Cows on Parade, a bovine bunch that remind the city of its meat-processing past. Made of fiberglass, each of the 300 cows scattered around the city for the event boasted a distinctive dress, an original design, or even a disguise.

Inspired by a similar exhibit in Switzerland, shoe entrepreneur Peter Hanig paired up with Chicago Cultural Affairs Commissioner Lois Weisberg to bring the horned cows to Chicago. Artists were invited to choose from cows in three different poses and decorate theirs as they pleased, so the herd is incredibly varied in style.

After the event, many of the cows were auctioned off for charity and went on to greener pastures. But a few of them have lingered. See if you can find the cows still parading around at the following locations in the city.

Look for the red *Swiss Cow* (310 W. Dickens Avenue) and the muted yet colorful *W. la Vaca 1999 #2* by artist Virginio Ferrari (atrium lobby of 20 N. Michigan Avenue). Hanig himself donated the elegant *Bronze Cow* to the city of Chicago as a reminder of the original event. It now graces the entrance to the Chicago Cultural Center (78 E. Washington Street). Other cows to be found include *Vaca Victoria, Bessie, Holy Cow,* and *Cowlileo.*

> **TIP:** See if you can spot *Cowlileo*, who gazes up at the stars via his telescope, near the entrance to the 606 Biking Trail at 1808 N. Damen Avenue.

Address Various (see map) //
Getting there Varies by
location of each cow // Hours
Unrestricted // Ages 3+

22__CRICKET HILL

Kids and kites

Reaching 45 feet high, archetypal Cricket Hill is a year-round playground for the kids of Chicago. In the springtime, it's the perfect place to catch a gust of wind and fly a spectacular kite into the clouds. In the summer, roll yourself into a dizzy spell down its grassy green sides, giggling all the way down.

Nestled between Montrose Avenue Beach and Lake Shore Drive, Cricket Hill is a sporting hill surrounded by sporting fields. Eventually, it morphed into an unofficial hippy-dippy gathering spot. When the Grateful Dead's Jerry Garcia died, thousands of Deadheads congregated on the hill in tribute. Every May, the children of Chicago step out into the sunshine, climb Cricket Hill, and harness the winds of our windy city at the Kids & Kites Festival, an annual tradition established by our former mayor and kite enthusiast, Richard M. Daley. This uniquely Chicago-style event brings some of the largest and most uniquely shaped kites to the wide expanse of blue sky. On-hand experts are happy to teach little ones how to catch a breeze and soar. One of the most popular highlights of the festival is the Big Kite Candy Drop, which is a piñata-like kite filled with candies that drop from the sky, and kids scramble to grab the treats.

Come winter, it's the best sledding hill in the city. Year round, its peak offers sweeping views of the skyline and lakefront.

Don't forget to bring a blanket and pack a picnic. Plenty of trees at the base of the hill provide welcome shade.

TIP: www.ChicagoKite.com is the go-to place for kites of all shapes and sizes, including kites for flyers of all levels, from beginners to pros.

Address 4500 N. Lake Shore Drive at W. Montrose, Chicago, IL 60607, www.chicagoparkdistrict.com/parks-facilities/cricket-hill // Getting there Red Line to Wilson, then CTA bus 136 or 146 to Marine Drive & Montrose // Hours Daily 6am–11pm // Ages 3+

23_ CROWN FOUNTAIN

Chicago's unofficial downtown water park

When the Crown Fountain was unveiled to the public in 2004, few expected that Millennium Park's latest art installation would become Chicago's unofficial downtown water park.

In 1999, the Crown family agreed to sponsor a fountain for the new park and held an informal design competition. Spanish artist Jaume Plensa's video sculpture-style fountain installation, ultra-modern yet inspired by Europe's earliest public fountains, won.

Two 50-foot LED towers project video images of the faces of diverse Chicago citizens, replacing the gargoyles common in medieval European fountains. Plensa looked for volunteers from community organizations. Ultimately, he found over 1,000 people who agreed to be photographed and to share their likenesses with everyone who would visit the fountain for years to come. As reported by The Block Club in 2017, the photos will always be the same. So you'll see familiar faces whenever you visit. Every few minutes, a stream pours from their digital mouths, perfect for cooling oneself on a hot summer day. The towers are separated by a 232-foot-long stretch of black granite, where children gather to splash and play, breaking the images of the faces, sky, and city that reflect upon the 1/8-inch-deep pool.

In a 2017 interview with Chicago Gallery News, Plensa noted that he always checks in with his unique fountain whenever he finds himself in Chicago "to be sure that it still exists... I'm really happy because people completely embrace the piece, and it's not anymore mine."

TIP: Millennium Park's Lurie Garden's dramatically lit, 15-foot-high 'shoulder' hedge is a physical representation of Carl Sandburg's famous description of the "City of Big Shoulders."

Address 201 E. Randolph Street,
Chicago, IL 60602,
www.millenniumparkfoundation.org //
Getting there Brown, Orange, Purple,
Green, or Pink Line to Adams/Wabash //
Hours Daily 6am–11pm // Ages 3+

24_ CTA HOLIDAY TRAIN

Santa's Chicago-style sleigh

When he's not flying merrily around the world on his enchanted sleigh, Santa Claus loves public transportation. For over 25 years, he heads to the Windy City, pre-holidays, and rolls his very own sleigh-style CTA train onto the city's tracks. This one-of-kind, joyful tradition gives all the good boys and girls of Chicago, as well as visitors to our fair city, the chance to share a wish list with the big man in red before he heads back to the North Pole for toy pick up and sets off on his magical Christmas Eve journey.

The holiday train tradition began with an out-of-service Blue Line train. It hosted a humble "Season's Greetings from the CTA" placard on its front when it began working overtime during the holidays, delivering food to various charities. To this day, the CTA Holiday Train brings joy to both unsuspecting and eager passengers, while also continuing to deliver food baskets to various family-focused charitable agencies throughout the city, in the true spirit of the season.

It's impossible to not be swept away by the spirit of Christmas as the CTA Holiday Train pulls into the station, decked out in thousands of twinkling lights. Santa's elves ride in their special workshop train inside. It's positively packed with all the trimmings and trappings of Christmas – even the poles are transformed into candy canes. Head honcho Santa Claus' sleigh is perched on an open-air flatcar, decked out in Christmas trees, his merry reindeer leading the way, but any of the elves are happy to pass him a note in case you're eager to share your Christmas wish list.

The CTA Holiday Train hits each of the L rail lines in turn from the end of November to around Christmas Eve. All aboard from some early Christmas cheer.

Address CTA Transit, www.transitchicago.com/holidayfleet // Getting there All L lines, normal fees apply // Hours See website for schedule // Ages 3+

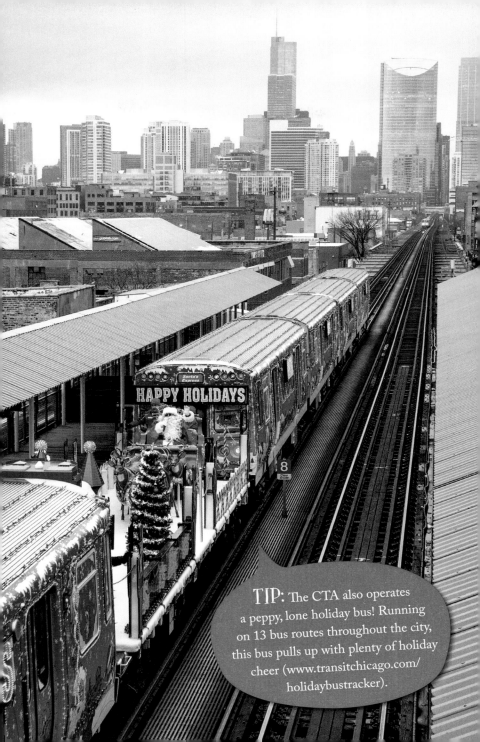

TIP: The CTA also operates a peppy, lone holiday bus! Running on 13 bus routes throughout the city, this bus pulls up with plenty of holiday cheer (www.transitchicago.com/holidaybustracker).

25_ DAVE'S DOWN TO EARTH ROCK SHOP

Hidden gems

Dave Douglass was always fascinated by rocks. Big rocks. Small rocks. Minerals. Fossils. So he opened Dave's Down to Earth Rock Shop in 1970 at the age of 20.

Then Dave met his Sandy, who shared his passion for rocks. The rockin' duo traveled far and wide, across the western United States, Canada, and Mexico, as they searched for rare rocks. They amassed such a large collection of rare fossils that they turned the basement of their shop into the David and Sandra Douglass Prehistoric Life Museum and opened it to the public.

The shop's main floor is packed with rocks and minerals galore in every size, shape, and color on planet Earth. Prices can go up to thousands of dollars, but they start at 50 cents, making it easy to start a little rock collection of your own. A wall covered in bead-sized minerals and gems gives visitors the opportunity to make a one-of-a-kind, affordable bracelet or necklace on-site.

Step down into the basement and back in time to the mid-Pennsylvanian epoch, 309 million years ago, when the fossils here were once living flora and fauna. Of special note are the fossils collected at the Mazon Creek area here in Illinois, many of which Dave collected while growing up. Dig around and see if you can find the complete cave bear skeleton from France, insects frozen in time from Mexico, and the fossilized crab from Italy.

> TIP: Listen to the fossils of the music world – used LPs, 45s, and CDs at Squeezebox Books and Music.

Address 711 Main Street, Evanston, IL 60202, +1 (847) 866-7374, www.davesrockshop.com, rockshop1@att.net // Getting there Metra UP-N to Main Street Station Evanston // Hours See website // Ages 3+

26_DAVID M. MCKAY MEMORIAL GARDEN

Shall I compare thee to a summer's day?

Childhood is fleeting, a fact that every parent of a young adult knows all too well.

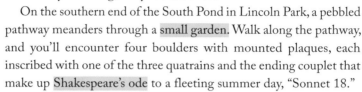

The days are long; the years are short.

On the southern end of the South Pond in Lincoln Park, a pebbled pathway meanders through a small garden. Walk along the pathway, and you'll encounter four boulders with mounted plaques, each inscribed with one of the three quatrains and the ending couplet that make up Shakespeare's ode to a fleeting summer day, "Sonnet 18."

David McKay grew up in north suburban Winnetka. In the summer of 2002, he passed away at the tender age of 22. In a 2011 interview with *Chicago Tribune* columnist Mary Schmich, McKay's mother Jackie described how she had tried to heal with long walks in Lincoln Park. One day she chanced upon the then-unkempt park and read the timeless sonnet. "It seemed to me to be a celebration of youth," she told Schmich. "It spoke about having life end too soon. It was very comforting to me." In memory of her beloved son, she offered to fix up and maintain the park.

Introduce the English poet by walking along the pathway and reading the sonnet to your child. There are benches, perfect for enjoying a picnic in the sunshine, amidst the flowers, some of which are mentioned by Shakespeare in his many sonnets and plays, and indulge in the beauty of Lincoln Park, where "summer's lease hath all too short a date."

TIP: Pick up picnic provisions at the Green City Market, Chicago's premier, all-organic market, which pops up near the Farm-in-the-Zoo, every Wednesday and Saturday, May–October (near 1817 N. Clark Street).

Address Southern edge of the South Pond of Lincoln Park, 2025 N. Lincoln Park W., Chicago, IL 60614 // Getting there Brown or Purple Line to Sedgwick // Hours Daily 6am–11pm // Ages 3+

27_DIGITAL YOUTH MEDIA LAB

HOMAGO hub

The Art Deco Chicago Bee is an icon of the South Side neighborhood of Bronzeville, built by wealthy entrepreneur Anthony Overton to house his *Chicago Bee*, a weekly newspaper that showcased the happenings of the vibrant community from 1925 to 1947. Indeed it was an editor of the *Bee*, James Gentry, who coined the term 'Bronzeville' to describe this epicenter of business and culture built by African Americans newly arriving from the South.

Transformed into a library in 1996, today's Chicago Bee Branch Library melds Bronzeville history and modern-day technology. The result: Digital Youth Media Lab, a space that invites kids to HOMAGO (Hang Out, Mess Around, and Geek Out) while creating music, video, 2D and 3D design, photos, and podcasts.

Part of the Chicago Public Library's YOUmedia initiative, the library is a high-tech hub. Laptops with design and editing software, 3D printers, vinyl cutters, gaming systems, and of course, books, are just waiting to be used by creative kids. Perhaps the coolest spot in this tech-centered library is the dedicated audio recording studio, where kids are welcome to record their own music, podcasts, or voice-overs for video projects. Staff members are on hand to help teach the tech equipment ropes and guide kids as they plan and embark on their creative journies.

TIP: While in Bronzeville, pay a visit to the Monument to the Great Northern Migration – by sculptor Alison Saar.

Address 3647 S. State Street, Chicago, IL 60609, +1 (312) 747-6872, www.chipublib.org/locations/18, chicagobee@chipublib.org // Getting there Green Line to 35th-Bronzeville-IIT // Hours See website for library and YOUMedia hours // Ages 10+

Language

Noise Level

WORDS
ARE

IMPORTANT   EMPOWERING

VITAL   MEANINGFUL

It's okay to not
be okay !!!

28_DON CHURRO

Churros + champurrado = a match made in heaven

Churros have a murky origin story. Some say they were the invention of Spanish mountain shepherds. Others claim that Portuguese sailors brought back the recipe for *youtiao*, fried dough tubes, after an expedition to Northern China. The conquistadors carried the pastry tradition to Latin America.

Here in Chicago, we have Don Churro, our very own churro factory in the heart of Pilsen, a vibrant Mexican-American neighborhood that is home to both the National Museum of Mexican Arts and a rich tradition of murals. Don Churro churns out fresh churros daily, by the dozens and dozens. The long, choux-based pastries are fried on the spot, until they're perfectly golden and crispy.

Purists will want to go for the traditional churros, sprinkled with a simple dash of cinnamon sugar, but don't be afraid to give the many filled churros a try. Don Churro offers churros filled with Bavarian cream, chocolate, guava, cream cheese, strawberry, and *cajeta*, a *dulce de leche*-style caramel.

Cookies pair with milk. Donuts are best dipped in coffee. Churros are best friends with champurrado, a warm, chocolate-based, cinnamon-spiced *atole* enriched with *masa de maíz* (corn flour). A classic Mexican drink, *champurrado* has been around since pre-Columbian times and was a favorite among both the Aztecs and Maya. Dip your churro in a steaming cup of *champurrado* to warm your heart, soul, and tummy.

> **TIP:** The National Museum of Mexican Art showcases the history and culture of both Mexico and Mexican communities in the United States. Museum entry is always free.

Address 1626 S. Blue Island Avenue, Chicago, IL 60608, +1 (312) 733-3173 // Getting there Pink Line to 18th Street // Hours Daily 6am–7pm // Ages 3+

29 _ DRAG QUEEN STORY HOUR

Express yourself

In a world filled with so much hate, it's more important than ever to teach our children tolerance, acceptance, and respect for all. On that note, how boring would this world be if everyone was the same?

The concept is simple: local drag queens volunteer to read inclusive, positive, fun, and thoughtful children's books at libraries, schools, and bookstores to kids who come to listen to stories. Children are usually first interested in the colors, energy, theatrics, and incredible style sense of these book-loving drag queens, but soon they're immersed in the tales at hand, just like any other story hour. Afterwards, the drag queen host will answer any and all questions and then lead an easy craft project or two.

"DQSH started a few years ago when Women and Children First started reaching out to area queens to come and read stories," said Muffy Fishbasket, Chicago's official story hour organizer. "I saw the need for it in Chicago and started to explore expanding it. I believe it's important to make our differences a normality. We are a part of these children's earliest memories, and they will take that with them throughout life. It's a small pebble, but the ripples will spread far."

At a recent story hour hosted at Albany Park library, drag queen Dixie Devereux read a collection of picture books to the children. "I think that anyone can appreciate a story time," shared Dixie. "For me it's important to show that drag queens are people, too."

> **TIP:** Check out *Pink is for Boys* by Robb Pearlman, a picture book that encourages girls and boys to enjoy what they love to do, whether it's racing cars or loving unicorns.

Michael Hall

Red
A Crayon's Story

WHERE
OLIVER
FITS

Cale Atkinson

Address Multiple venues,
www.muffyfishbasket.com/
story-time-with-drag-queens,
muffyfishbasket@gmail.com //
Getting there Varies //
Hours See website for locations
and schedules // Ages 3+

30_ DRAKE FAMILY SKYSCRAPER GALLERY

Meet Chicago's skyscrapers

Chicago is the birthplace of the skyscraper. The long-demolished Home Insurance Building, which sprang up on the northeast corner of LaSalle and Adams Streets in 1885, is considered the world's first skyscraper – its original 10 stories were a marvel at the time of its construction. From the early 1920s to the late 1930s, sky scraping buildings popped up across the city. The 108-story Willis Tower (formerly the Sears Tower) rose up 1,451 feet into the clouds in 1974 and remains the tallest building in the city today, with 44 fellow skyscrapers standing taller than 600 feet, making our city's skyline one of the most envied in the world.

On the second floor of the Chicago Architecture Center, the Drake Family Skyscraper Gallery is filled with scale models of Chicago's most famous skyscrapers, revealing what it takes to design and engineer these incredible architectural feats. From the Marina Towers to the John Hancock Center, this gallery gives kids the opportunity to see some of the most iconic buildings from every angle and is bound to inspire junior LEGO architects. In addition to Chicago high-rises, you'll also find models of famous skyscrapers from around the world, some of which are on loan from other museums.

Be sure to pop in to the Chicago Gallery, too, where the largest 3D model of the city's downtown area makes it easier to understand our city's rapid growth from river trading outpost to emerging megacity.

Address 111 E. Wacker Drive, Chicago, IL 60601, +1 (312) 922-8687, www.architecture.org, info@architecture.org // Getting there Red Line to Clark/Lake // Hours Daily 9:30am–5pm // Ages 5+

TIP: Blogger and photographer John Morris is recreating Chicago streets with paper miniatures at www.tinycity.net. The paper buildings are between one and two inches tall, with print-ready plans so you can make a city of your own.

31_DULCELANDIA

Piñata paradise

No Mexican celebration is complete without a piñata, a tradition that likely began to honor the birthday of the Aztec god Huītzilōpōchtli.

At Dulcelandia, kids can take their pick from an endless array of piñatas. Over 100 are on display, dressed up in their papier-mâché best as every movie or television character, animal, and even political figure under the sun. Unicorns, llamas, donkeys, and dragons share space with Batman, Mickey and Minnie, Spiderman, Super Mario, and Donald Trump. Star-shaped piñatas are made for tiny tots – they don't need to be struck with a stick, as they feature an easy pull-string instead.

Since Dulcelandia is a wholesale distributor of Mexican candy in the Midwest, grab a basket and pack your piñata with traditional Mexican sweets.

Over 1,000 Mexican and American candies and chocolates are waiting to be discovered: try the *salsaghetti*, watermelon-flavored, spaghetti-shaped licorice that comes complete with a small packet of tamarind 'sauce' to pour on top. The *Paleta MalvaBony Pop* is a milk-chocolate-coated marshmallow on a stick. Miniature tamarind caramels are wrapped in tiny corn husks. *Super Natilla* is a pecan toffee. The Pico Pepino Paleta is a cucumber-flavored lollipop with a chili kick. The *Dulce de Amaranto* is a Rice Krispy-style treat made with the ancient grain amaranth, a staple food of the Aztecs. Kids can taste the history of Mexico at Dulcelandia.

> **TIP:** Head across the street to La Perla Tapatia Bakery Jimenez for traditional Mexican pastries, cookies, bread, donuts, tortillas, tamales, and to-die-for tres leches cakes.

Address 3855 W. Fullerton Avenue, Chicago, IL 60647, +1 (773) 235-7825, www.dulcelandia.com, info@dulcelandia.com // **Getting there** Red Line to Fullerton or Blue Line to California, then CTA bus 74 to Fullerton/Springfield // **Hours** Mon–Fri 10am–8pm, Sat 9am–8pm, Sun 10am–7pm // **Ages** 3+

32_ ELK HERD
Meet the Wapiti

Elk Grove Village wasn't just a pretty name chosen for this planned suburban community. Incorporated in 1956, few people know that an actual small elk herd calls this corner of Chicagoland home.

In 1925, nine cows and one bull were delivered by train from Yellowstone National Park to what was a small farming community. Today, three cows, one adult bull, and two male calves live in a 17-acre enclosed pasture located within the 3,700-acre Busse Woods.

Once upon a time, about 10 million elk roamed the northern two-thirds of North America. The First Nations named them wapiti. Then the Europeans arrived, and unregulated hunting, livestock, habitat destruction, urbanization, and westward expansion decreased their population to only about 100,000.

Each year, the Chicago Zoological Society conducts health workups on the herd. Every three to four years, the team introduces new males to maintain genetic diversity.

Despite their huge antlers – elk antlers can grow up to one inch per day – their brown coats make it easy for them to blend into the woods, and they can be difficult to spot at times.

Hike around the perimeter of their pen treading lightly, however, and keep your eyes peeled. You're bound to spot a beautiful elk grazing on the grasses, munching on tree bark or springtime sprouts, or resting among fallen trees. In the summertime, you might find them half-submerged in a pool of water – that's how they cool off and avoid the biting insects.

TIP: While you're in Busse Woods, bike or hike the eight-mile Busse Forest Paved Trail (www.traillink.com/trail/busse-woods-trail), which runs in part along the elk pen. More than 30 groves are perfect for picnicking.

Address 225 N. Arlington
Heights Road, Elk Grove
Village, IL 60007,
+1 (800) 870-3666,
www.fpdcc.com/
busse-woods // Getting
there Blue Line to
Rosemont, then CTA
bus 606 to Woodfield
Corporate Center; Green
Line to Harlem/Lake,
then CTA bus 757 to
King/Northwest Point
Boulevard // Hours
See website for seasonal
hours // Ages 3+

33__FABYAN WINDMILL

Riverbank idyll

Colonel George and Nellie Fabyan were delightfully eccentric millionaires. Mr. Fabyan managed his father's textile business while also pursuing the study of modern cryptography, the art of writing or solving codes. The couple purchased a farmhouse on the west bank of the Fox River Valley in the early 1900s and worked to transform 300-plus acres into their dream estate, Riverbank.

In addition to a Japanese-inspired garden, a private zoo, a Roman-style swimming pool, a lighthouse, endless gardens, grottoes, greenhouses, a farm, and a research laboratory, Fabyan felt he needed one more important feature to complete his grand estate: a windmill. In 1914, he purchased a 68-foot, 5-story structure originally built between 1850 and 1860 by Louis Blackhaus, a German craftsman, for about $8,000. He had it moved piece by piece from its original location to his grand estate in what is now Lombard, Illinois. Some of the pieces were so large and heavy that they had to be transported by a team of mules.

In the 1930s, the Forest Preserve District purchased Riverbank. In 1997, they contracted third-generation Dutch windmill maker Lucas Verbij to bring the windmill back to its working glory. Verbij noted, "The Fabyan Windmill is the best example of an authentic Dutch windmill in the United States. Actually, it's a treasure, and would be the most popular windmill in the Netherlands; we currently have 1,000 windmills. Restoring Fabyan Windmill was as much honor as it was duty." The newly functional windmill began operating in 2005 as one of the few in the world that are powered by good, old-fashioned, natural wind energy.

Address Crissey Avenue, Batavia, IL 60510, +1 (630) 208-8662, www.bikingbatavia.org/maps-routes // Getting there Metra to Geneva, IL // Hours See website for windmill hours and tours // Ages 3+

TIP: Rent adult and kid bikes at Mill Race Cyclery, located about 15 minutes by foot from the station, to explore the windmill and the scenic Fox River Trail.

34_ FANNY'S BEDROOM

Glimpse into the life of a Gilded Age girl

Fanny Glessner was born on March 25, 1878, the only daughter of John Glessner, a newly rich industrialist, and his wife, Frances. Fanny grew up in the family's pink granite, castle-like home on posh Prairie Avenue, once an exclusive enclave and home to other early influential Chicagoans, including Marshall Field and George Pullman. Considered the residential masterpiece of 19th-century architect H. H. Richardson, the grand yet cozy Glessner House, where Fanny grew up, remains frozen in time. Filled with original furnishings, the mansion offers a glimpse back to Gilded Age Chicago.

Fanny's bedroom was just recently restored, thanks to the return of her circa 1887 bed by Glessner family descendants and a generous anonymous gift. Her elegant 'artichoke' bed covering was most likely embroidered by the Royal School of Needlework in London. *FG* is carved on the face of the center drawer of her desk, custom built for her in 1894 by A. H. Davenport & Co. Her kid-sized bureau was made by Isaac Scott for her 4th birthday. Atop the bureau are two sweet photos of Fanny herself. A 'secret entrance' leads through her beloved brother's closet and into his bedroom.

Fanny's mom described her daughter as a delightful, clever, and precocious little girl. She was homeschooled, along with her brother, here at the Glessner House. Indeed, little Fanny would go on to become the 'Mother of Modern C.S.I.' She created miniature crime scenes, the *Nutshell Studies of Unexplained Death*, which became an essential tool in teaching early seminars on homicide scene investigation. Not only did she also help to establish the Department of Legal Medicine at Harvard University, she also became the first ever female police captain in the United States.

Address 1800 S. Prairie Avenue, Chicago, IL 60616, +1 (312) 326-1480, www.glessnerhouse.org, info@glessnerhouse.org // Getting there Metra to 18th Street // Hours Wed–Sun 11am–4pm // Ages 3+

TIP: To see inside another ornate Gilded Age mansion, visit Nickerson House, which has been restored and now hosts the Driehaus Museum of art, architecture, and design of the late 19th century to the present.

35__FANTASY COSTUMES

Embrace your inner character

Are you in urgent need of a swamp monster suit? A child-sized Benjamin Franklin wig? A set of hairy werewolf hands? An adhesive handlebar mustache? Customized vampire fangs? Fantasy Costumes has you covered. This amazing, oversized shop, located in the historic Six Corners shopping district, offers an entire city block packed with over one million fanciful outfits, as well as wigs, masks, and makeup for every season and creative reason.

If you're looking for Halloween costume inspiration, or you are hoping to take on a new superpower persona, you'll find hundreds of ideas among the merchandise, which fills every corner, nook, cranny, and crevice from floor to ceiling. It's easy to get lost as you explore the many crowded rooms, each dedicated to a costume element, including masks, makeup, wigs, hats, and so on. But the creative team members here, who are also known to hide behind boxes and pop out to scare customers, will point you in the right direction. In the two weeks leading up to the scariest day of the year, a.k.a. Halloween, Fantasy Costumes is conveniently open 24 hours a day. Not looking to make a huge investment? Fantasy Costumes will rent you everything you need to transform into your fave character of the moment.

Fantasy Costumes' mission hasn't changed over the last five decades: "We strive to help customers look great while having fun. And it's OK to get a little crazy."

> TIP: The nearby National Veterans Art Museum highlights the impact of war through art inspired by combat and created by veterans.

Address 4065 N. Milwaukee Avenue, Chicago, IL 60641, +1 (773) 777-0222, www.fantasycostumes.com // Getting there Blue Line to Montrose // Hours Mon–Sat 9:30am–8pm, Sun 11am–5pm // Ages 3+

36_ FILBERT'S SODA POP FACTORY

Sip the rainbow

Trivia time! Can you guess which old-school soda is made from the bark of the sassafras tree?

In the late 1800s, George Filbert delivered milk, ice, and coal by horse-drawn wagon to homes in the South Side Bridgeport neighborhood. George's son, Charlie, loved root beer and was just in time for Prohibition when he created his very own recipe for the root-sourced, alcohol-free drink. The family began rolling out half barrels of a one-of-a-kind, draft-style root beer.

More than 90 years later, fourth-generation family member Ron Filbert continues to make his family's famous root beer from the same South Side soda pop factory.

Not only can you count on having a taste of old Chicago via their namesake brew, you can also watch it get bottled on-site in this factory that looks pretty much the same as it did when it began selling the popular bubbly beverage in the Roaring Twenties. Tap your feet to the melodic tune of glass bottles traveling along the old assembly line. First, they're filled with sweet, colorful soda flavors. Then they're capped, labeled, and packed in boxes for delivery across the city.

In addition to its classic Chicago Root Beer, Filbert's also produces a rainbow of fizzy sodas – over 25 flavors, from apple to watermelon. So grab an empty box and fill it up with a selection that will quench your thirst for *pop*, the word Chicagoans use to describe the sugary sodas that made Filbert's famous throughout the decades.

Address 3430 S. Ashland Avenue, Chicago, IL 60608, +1 (773) 847-1520, www.filbertsrootbeer.com, ronfilbert@filbertsrootbeer.com // Getting there Orange Line to Ashland // Hours Mon–Fri 8am–4pm, Sat 9am–1pm // Ages 3+

TIP: After you fill up on soda, dig into a bowl of chili at Lindy's Chili, a South Side favorite since 1924.

37_ FIREWORKS FLOAT

The best seat in the house

The most magical bi-weekly event of the summer is always the fireworks spectacular that launches from Navy Pier, every Wednesday at 9:30pm and Saturday at 10:15pm. Each brilliant show lasts 10 to 15 action-packed minutes. While you can always catch the fireworks from the pier, a rooftop deck, or the nearby shoreline, the best seat in the house is without a doubt from a tandem kayak gently rocking on the Lake Michigan waves, directly beneath the action.

Kayak Chicago offers a family-friendly 'Fireworks Float,' perfect for families that are new to kayaking and experienced paddlers. Everyone will begin with a lesson in paddle strokes, safety, and rules of the water, so you have the skills to feel comfortable in your kayak and fully prepared for your three-hour adventure. With lights on your kayaks, you'll paddle out from North Avenue Beach, follow the shoreline at a leisurely pace, then raft up as a group, and enjoy the best view of the fireworks in the city.

Some athletic ability is recommended, but no experience is required. Any age can paddle in a tandem kayak with an adult, but kids need to be at least 12 in order to paddle a single kayak on their own, still accompanied by an adult in a separate kayak. Dress prepared to get a little wet and bring a water bottle and snacks for the journey.

As you paddle back to the shore, be sure to look up at the night sky: you just might catch a glimpse of a falling star!

Address N. Avenue Beach, 1600 N. Lake Shore Drive, Chicago, IL 60613, +1 (312) 852-9258, www.kayakchicago.com, dave@kayakchicago.com // **Getting there** Brown or Purple Line to Sedgwick // **Hours** Wed 7:15pm, Sat 8pm, Memorial Day–Labor Day // **Ages** 3+

TIP: Stand Up Paddle boarding, or SUP, is another fun and unique way to explore Lake Michigan. Kayak Chicago also offers an intro to SUP course and a shoreline tour.

38 _ FIRST DIVISION MUSEUM

Tank time at Cantigny Park

Hide from the enemy in a World War I trench. Man a landing craft as soldiers storm Omaha Beach on D-Day. Make your way through the treacherous jungles of Vietnam. Put on a headset and follow a soldier on a house raid in Iraq. At the First Division Museum at Cantigny Park, kids can experience the history of the 1st Infantry Division, the combined arms division of the United States Army, from World War I to the present day.

The 500-acre Cantigny Park was once the private country estate of *Chicago Tribune* publishing magnates Joseph Medill and his grandson Colonel Robert R. McCormick, who also served in World War I and saw action at the Battle of Cantigny. Today, its extensive formal and informal gardens, two museums, 27-hole golf course, picnic grove, playground, and hiking paths are all open to the public.

Dedicated to all those who have served and continue to serve, the museum's many interactive exhibits bring the sights, sounds, and soldiers' stories from World War I through modern times to a kid's level. Kids are even welcome to climb the extensive collection of tanks, armored vehicles, and artillery pieces located at 'Tank Park' on the grounds outside the museum.

Extend the learning at home and pick up a copy of *The First Division Museum Coloring Book*, which offers detailed sketches and descriptions that explore the history of the Big Red One, or the 1st Infantry Division of the United States Army, available in the museum gift shop.

TIP: Hike the 2.5-mile Wood Chip Trail (www.alltrails.com/trail/us/illinois/wood-chip-trail-loop), which begins next to 'Tank Park' in front of the First Division Museum.

Address 1s151 Winfield Road, Wheaton, IL 60189, +1 (630) 260-8185, www.fdmuseum.org // Getting there Travel west on I-290 to exit I-290 at the East-West tollway (I-88) west interchange; take I-88 west and exit at Winfield Road; go north on Winfield Road // Hours See website // Ages 3+

39_ FIRST NATIONS GARDEN

Healing and hope in bloom

In spring 2019, two tipis – one about 20 feet tall, the other half that height – rose from the ground of a formerly vacant lot in Albany Park. With hopes of bringing healing to the Native American community in Chicago, the Chi-Nations Youth Council, which advocates for Native youth, partnered with the American Indian Center to create the First Nations Garden, a dedicated space where urban youth of Native American ancestry and others willing to learn can gather, grow their own food and medicine, and heal both body and spirit.

The garden offers an excellent opportunity to introduce children to the Native American community that thrives within the city. Chicago is the ancestral home of the Ojibwe, Odawa, and Potawatomi peoples. Today, 65,000 people who identify as Native American live in the area, the third largest urban Native American population in the country, according to the 2010 US Census.

The tipis in the garden are reminiscent of the days before the big city of Chicago was even a distant dream. A community garden with a focus on healing fruits, veggies, and herbs, is tended by members of the Chi-Nations Youth Council, who are often on hand to answer any questions and share the story of the garden efforts.

The garden has served as "a beacon for people, to let them know that there's still Native people here, especially in Albany Park," shared Anthony Tamez, Co-President of Chi-Nations Youth Council. A wigwam and a sweat lodge are set to rise in the near future.

Address 4599 N. Pulaski Road, Chicago, IL 60630, +1 (773) 275-5871, www.aicchicago.org/first-nations-community-garden, info@aicchicago.org // Getting there Blue Line to Irving Park, then CTA bus 53 to Pulaski & Wilson // Hours Daily dawn – dusk // Ages 3+

TIP: The Chi-Nations Youth Council hosts events, workshops, pow wows, and volunteer opportunities. Follow them on Facebook for updates and information (www.facebook.com/NativeYouth).

40_ FLYKID MURALS

You're so fly

Hebru Brantley's gallery is the city of Chicago. His iconic, superpower-charged characters pop up on unsuspecting walls across the city, from north to south, east to west.

Flyboy, a little boy with vintage aviator goggles and always on the brink of flying into an adventure, appears often in Brantley's work. Inspired by the Tuskegee Airmen, Brantley told *DNAInfo* in 2013 that he created the character "out of a need to have heroes of color, whether Black, Asian, or White, European."

Flyboy Uptown seems as if he's flying right on past the Uptown Broadway Building. A group of five Flykids explore the world beneath the bridge at 1800-1802 Pratt Boulevard. A Flygirl with neon pink pigtails and bright, blue goggles gazes towards the future from a mural at 1395 North Wood.

Born and raised in Bronzeville, Brantley used art to keep himself focused, avoiding gang life. Today he's recognized nationally for his public works and solo shows. Icons like Chance the Rapper, Lenny Kravitz, and George Lucas are fans of his work. Jay-Z bought one of his paintings right on the spot at Art Basel for $20,000.

See how many of Brantley's pop art, comic book-style, grand-scale murals you can spot around town. Run with the kids in *Nike Running* at N. Damen Avenue and Concord Place in Bucktown. And power into outer space with Flyboy, whom you'll find blasting off from a mural at 2019 N. Mendell Street.

> TIP: Go on a street art scavenger hunt! Pick a neighborhood and see how many public murals you can find. Note the artists' names and look them up later to learn their stories.

Address Various, see map and visit
www.hebrubrantley.com // Getting there
Various // Hours Unrestricted // Ages 3+

41_ GALLOPING GHOST ARCADE

Back to the '80s

The Golden Age of Arcade Games began in 1978 with the release of *Space Invaders* and hit new heights with the release of *Pac-Man* in 1980. Pac-Mania led kids in droves to local arcades across the US Saturday Supercade, the 1983 animated television series produced for Saturday mornings, introduced beloved video game characters Frogger, Donkey Kong, Donkey Kong Jr., Kangaroo, Pitfall Harry, and Space Ace to the masses.

Then personal computers and video game consoles came along and ruined all the fun.

However, hidden like a ghost in suburban Brookfield, Pac Man can still be found eating pellets, Donkey Kong continues to climb vines towards greatness, and Mario and Luigi haven't given up yet with their attempts to rescue Princess Toadstool.

When owner Doc Mack opened Galloping Ghost in 2010, he saved many of the arcade greats from extinction. To this day, Mack is constantly restoring and reintroducing old favorites while also keeping space for newcomers to the gaming scene. Almost 700 electronic games are waiting to be played by kids and kids at heart. Note, however, that old-school video games weren't rated. *Ms. Pac Man*, the *Teenage Mutant Ninja Turtles*, and *Peter Pack Rat* mingle with *Tecmo Knight*, *Robocop*, and *Zombie Raiders*.

TIP: Doc Mack's ever-expanding collection of 30-plus pinball games is now housed two blocks east of Galloping Ghost. $30 gives you unlimited play at both arcades.

Forget stuffing your pockets with quarters. Galloping Ghost is a coin- and token-free arcade. $20 gets you all day, unlimited play in the largest arcade in the country.

Address 9415 Ogden Avenue, Brookfield, IL 60513, +1 (708) 485-4700, www.gallopingghostarcade.com // Getting there Metra BNSF to Brookfield // Hours Daily 11–2am // Ages 7+

42_ THE GARFIELD CENTRAL

All aboard this miniature railroad

 In the North Side neighborhood of Uptown, a train controlled by a state-of-the-art signaling system rambles along a track. This isn't the CTA's red line, however. This is the tiniest railroad in the city, built and operated by the Garfield Clarendon Model Railroad Club. Its 1,400 feet of hand-laid track winds through the fictional yet picturesque Appalachian towns of Summit, Georgetown, Bridgeport, and Williamsport. Miniature passengers wait for their train as tiny townspeople go about their daily business. Though small in stature, this is the biggest model train set in Chicago, offering a bird's-eye view of how freight and passenger trains – both small and big – operate.

The train engineers here are passionate about their hobby and eager to share the ins and outs of what it takes to conduct the railroad. Established in Garfield Park in 1947, the club moved to Clarendon Park in 1963, where it meets regularly in the field house. Construction of the elaborate, current model layout began in 1974. Featuring fully signaled, dual main lines and a two-car streetcar line, the train winds through both city and countryside scenery. It takes over 25 minutes at scale speed for a train to make a complete loop around the layout.

Operating sessions are always open to the public and typically occur the last Friday of the month at 7pm. The club also conducts open houses four times a year. Check their website for details on upcoming train-related events.

Address 4501 N. Clarendon Avenue, Chicago, IL 60640, +1 (773) 609-2788, www.garfieldcentral.org // Getting there Purple or Red Line to Wilson // Hours Last Friday of each month, 7–9pm // Ages 3+

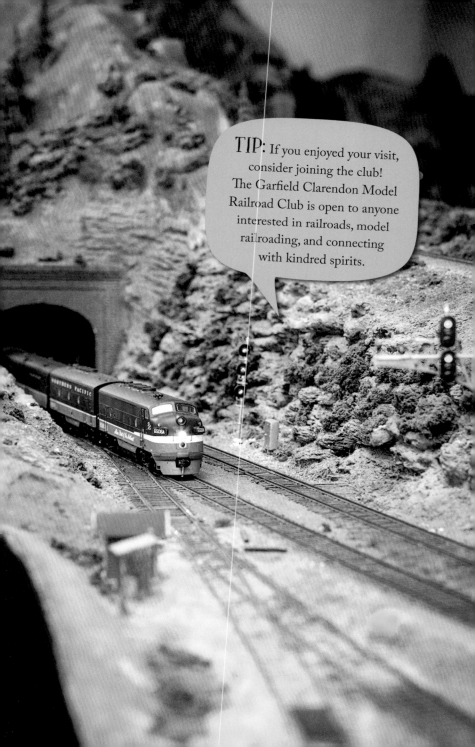

43_ GIRAFFE FEEDING EXPERIENCE

Beware of the 20-inch-long tongue

The giraffe is the tallest animal in the world, with an average height reaching up to 20 feet. At about six feet, their legs alone are twice as tall as most kids. With a whopping four stomachs to fill, they also love to eat. In fact, they spend their entire day eating. It takes a while to eat the 75 pounds of food that they typically consume every day. Despite their impressive stature, a giraffe's neck is too short to reach the ground, so they depend on trees – or a few friendly kids – when it comes to dining.

At Brookfield Zoo, kids can help a giraffe dig into a leafy buffet. For a small fee, kids can purchase and feed these magnificent creatures a tasty treat, such as romaine lettuce or kale, as well as leaves, twigs, and branches cut down and delivered by ComEd from trees trimmed along overhead power lines. You will stand on a short wooden box and await the giraffes, who will meander over at the sight of a snack then lower their long necks to bite the goods in your outstretched hand. Just beware of their very long tongues, which stretch 18–20 inches!

An animal care specialist is on hand to educate guests about how the zoo is supporting conservation efforts of reticulated giraffes in Africa, so come prepared with plenty of questions and be ready to learn a few fun facts about these incredible animals.

Giraffe encounters are offered daily between Memorial Day and Labor Day from 11am to 2pm on a first come, first served basis until all the greens are gone.

TIP: Every day, the zoo hosts a number of Zoo Chats. A zookeeper will bring an animal out for a chat and kids can sometimes even pet their new scaly, feathered, or furry friend.

Address Brookfield
Zoo, 8400 W. 31st
Street, Brookfield,
IL 60513,
+1 (708) 688-8000,
www.czs.org //
Getting there Metra
BNSF to Hollywood
(Zoo Stop) // Hours
Daily 10am–5pm //
Ages 3+

44_ GOAT CHILLS

Pastoral bliss at GlennArt Farm

It's the least likely place in the world where you'd expect to find pastoral bliss, but smack dab in the middle of Chicago's West Side, GlennArt Farm has managed to carve out an almost idyllic, country-like space. Families are invited to chill with the most lovable goat herd in the city.

Owners Carolyn and David Ioder, who both descend from Midwestern farming families, launched the farm in 2011. During high season from April through November, the couple makes cheese and milks goats seven days a week while also selling their organic eggs and honey. But it's their herd of dairy goats that draws in the most visitors when the small farm hosts yoga classes and 'goat chills.'

Goat Chill participants simply hang out in the pasture with the super sociable goats. Feed them delicious, goat-approved snacks, give them a good back scratch (goats don't like to be petted but always enjoy a good back scratch), and relish in their endless affection and extreme silliness. Warning: grumpy folks are bound to crack a smile when spending time with this herd.

The goats live primarily in their large pen, but in the summer, they head out daily, *en masse*, through the alley and to the large lot one block east of the house, where they enjoy grazing on wild grasses and plants. Goat yoga, also open to kids, is hosted here in the middle of the small field, where nature has reclaimed its glory, ignoring the urban grit and grime, blooming amidst the concrete and construction.

"Kids of a goat kind like to play and check out new things," said David. "Kids of a human kind do too, and they develop a greater appreciation for nature."

Address 5749 W. Midway Park, Chicago, IL 60644, +1 (847) 612-7315, www.glennartfarm.com, glennartfarm@gmail.com // Getting there Green Line to Austin // Hours See website for hours and reservations // Ages 3+

TIP: Become a member of GlennArt Farm's Goat Guardian Guild, and you'll receive six free quarts of raw goat milk and invitations to special events. Best of all, you'll have the opportunity to name newborn baby goats (kids)!

45_GOSPEL BRUNCH

Feed your soul at the House of Blues

Born in the 1930s at the Pilgrim Baptist Church on Chicago's South Side, gospel music has roots in American folk, African-American spirituals, and early blues and jazz. It's the only musical genre that promises to soothe your soul, lift your spirits, and transform a lingering bad attitude into a sense of gratitude. The 'World Famous Gospel Brunch' at the House of Blues serves up energizing, Chicago-style gospel with a tried and true Southern brunch, making it the hottest Sunday service in town.

In Chicago, Thomas Andrew Dorsey, a.k.a. the 'Father of Gospel Music,' recorded many of the most celebrated gospel songs of all times, including, "I'm Going to Live the Life I Sing About in My Song" and "Take My Hand, Precious Lord." Kids will be tapping their toes, stomping their feet, swirling their napkins, and singing along to Dorsey's classics and newer hits, all performed by a local gospel singing choir in the eclectic main theater, which has the vibe of a museum as it's decked out in over 700 pieces of folk art from across the US.

The stars of the endless, all-you-can-eat buffet are the House of Blues' 'world famous' fried chicken & waffles and biscuits & gravy. But the omelet station, carving station complete with prime rib and roasted chicken, and complimentary mimosas and coffee ensure that everyone in the family finds their favorites.

The entire preacher-led show is filled with audience interaction and awesome music. Enthusiastic kids will have a chance to hit the stage and belt out a refrain or two on the mic.

Address 329 N. Dearborn Street, Chicago, IL 60654, +1 (312) 923-2000, www.houseofblues.com/chicago // Getting there Brown or Purple Line to Merchandise Mart // Hours Sun 10:30am & 12:30pm // Ages 5+

TIP: Burn off the biscuits with a ping pong match or a round of bowling at 10Pin, located next to the House of Blues.

46_ GRAUE MILL MUSEUM

There is a season (turn, turn, turn)

Since 1852, the Graue Mill has been grinding cornmeal, its waterwheel turning on the banks of the picturesque Salt Creek. Today, the Graue Mill Museum is dedicated to bridging past and present through living-history programs, including milling, spinning, and weaving demonstrations that illustrate the daily life of a time when water, not electricity, was a common power source.

Friedrich Graue was born in Germany but emigrated to what was once the farming village of Fullersburg, Illinois. As Pietist Germans, Graue and his family opposed American slavery, and the mill is one of three authenticated Illinois stops on the Underground Railroad. Legend has it that President Abraham Lincoln visited Graue Mill when traveling from Chicago to Springfield.

On the main floor, kids can help grind corn using Miller Graue's grand buhrstones. On the second and third floors, volunteers in period clothing demonstrate spinning and weaving and talk about life in Civil War days. A children's bedroom showcases the everyday life of the Graue kids. Head down to the cellar where the giant wooden gear system that operates the grindstone turns slowly to the tune of the river. The Graue family once hid fugitive slaves here as they made their way to freedom, a fact explained in the exhibit *The Underground Railroad in DuPage County*.

Make sure to follow the short hiking trail linking the Graue Mill to the Fullersburg Nature Center, the interactive, mini-nature museum located at the end of the trail.

Address 3800 York Road, Oak Brook, IL 60523, +1 (630) 655-2090, www.grauemill.org, info@grauemill.org // Getting there York Road, 0.25 mile north of Ogden Avenue, at the junction of York and Spring Roads // Hours See website for seasonal hours // Ages 3+

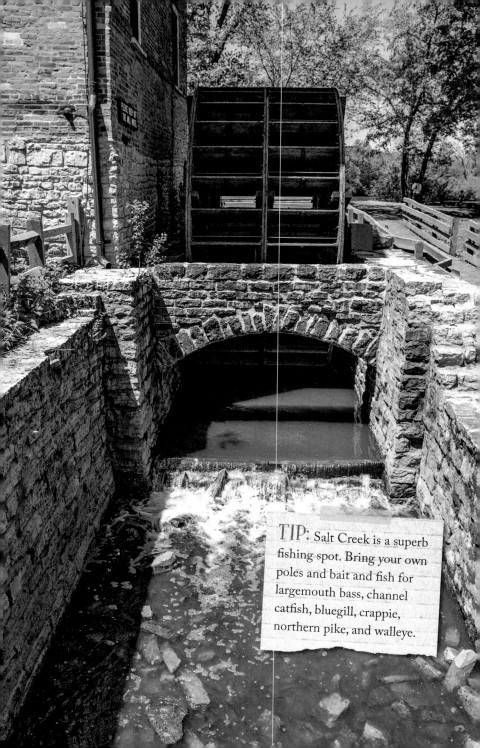

TIP: Salt Creek is a superb fishing spot. Bring your own poles and bait and fish for largemouth bass, channel catfish, bluegill, crappie, northern pike, and walleye.

47_ GRAVE OF INEZ CLARKE

Beware of wandering ghosts at Graceland Cemetery

Established in 1860, Graceland Cemetery is not only the final resting place of many illustrious early citizens... it's also one of the most paranormally active sites in Chicago.

Don't be surprised if you catch sight of a ghostly little girl wandering the grounds, dressed in her Victorian best, umbrella in hand.

Legend has it that six-year-old Inez Clarke was enjoying a picnic with her family all the way back in 1880, when a thunderstorm quickly blew over Lake Michigan and into town. Suddenly, she was struck by lightning, dying before her parents' very own eyes. Devastated, they topped her grave with a beautiful, white marble statue of the beloved, vivacious little girl they remembered.

Little Inez sits on a small chair, with a sweet smile on her face, frozen in time. She carries an umbrella in her hand and is enclosed in a glass case, perhaps to protect her spirit from yet another rogue thunderstorm or lightning strike.

Spirit-sensitive cemetery visitors report that sometimes little Inez's restless ghost steps out of her grave and her enclosed glass case to wander the cemetery, especially on stormy nights. Sometimes, it's said, you can hear her crying in the wee hours of the night. An old watchman confirmed that he once found her glass box empty while he was out walking the grounds during a thunderstorm.

Cemetery visitors often leave small trinkets for Inez. Perhaps she just wants to come out of her eternal rest and play...

Address 4001 N. Clark Street, Chicago, IL 60613, +1 (773) 525-1105, www.gracelandcemetery.org, info@gracelandcemetery.org // Getting there Red Line to Sheridan // Hours Mon–Fri 8am–4pm, Sat & Sun 9am–4pm // Ages 3+

48_ GREEN HAIRY MONSTER

Guardian of the toys at the door

Beware of the hairy, green monster that lives in the West Loop. Approach his Racine Avenue residence with caution. Whenever he senses the smell of an approaching little kid, he heads straight to his massive front door and glares from behind the windowpane, hoping to scare any potential toy robbers away with his gruff, green, hairy stare. Brave children who stand at his doorstep and peer into his googly eyes can expect to have their perspective magically altered.

Chances are you or your kids have played with a toy that grew out of the minds of some of the non-monsters who work in this playful building: Big Monster Toys designs, engineers, and prototypes toys and games for big names in the toy biz, like Mattel, Moose, Fisher-Price, and Hasbro to name a few.

Chicago has long been a toy-making town, and many of the most beloved and successful toys and games of the twentieth century were invented here, including *Mr. Machine*, *Lite Brite*, *Ants in the Pants*, *Operation*, *Mystery Date*, and *Simon*.

Founded in 1988 by three former partners of the legendary Chicago-based toy design firm Marvin Glass & Associates, Big Monster Toys stands as one of the few remaining toy manufacturers operating in the city. Their unique door is a brilliant reminder of the unexpected, unrequited joy of toys. For a truly Alice in Wonderland experience (and a great photo opp), see if you can jump up and grab the monster-sized doorknob.

TIP: You'll find a monster-sized red wagon just outside the headquarters of Radio Flyer, another iconic Chicago-based toy company, founded in 1917.

Address 21 S. Racine Avenue, Chicago, IL 60607, +1 (312) 829-8697, www.bmttoys.com, info@bmttoys.com // Getting there Blue Line to Racine // Hours Unrestricted // Ages 3+

49_ GROSSE POINT LIGHTHOUSE

Shine a little lighthouse light on me

In the 19th century, Chicago was a bustling port city. Schooners and then freight steamers streamed into the city, unloading their cargo on the docks of the Chicago River. Lake Michigan, however, was one of the most treacherous lakes to navigate. Out of the five Great Lakes, Lake Michigan has claimed the most lives in maritime disasters, and more than 1,500 ships have sunk into its depths.

One of the worst disasters on the lake occurred just offshore at Grosse Point in the early morning hours of September 8, 1860, when the passenger steamer *Lady Elgin* collided with a schooner. As the steamer began to break apart and sink, passengers struggled to reach land. An estimated 300 people drowned in the incident.

The citizens of Evanston, some of whom had witnessed the *Lady Elgin* disaster unfold, petitioned Congress for a lighthouse. Designed by Orlando Metcalfe Poe, United States Army officer and engineer in the American Civil War, who designed a number of other iconic Great Lakes' lighthouses, the Grosse Pointe Lighthouse was erected in 1873. Its beacon began warning ships of the shallow waters around the point and directing them safely into the Port of Chicago one year later.

The lighthouse stands 113 feet tall and is capped with a second order Fresnel lens, which can be seen up to 21 miles away. Take part in a guided tour, and you'll be able to climb all 141 steps to the tippy top, where you'll be rewarded with a memorable view of Lake Michigan, especially on clear, sunny days.

For safety reasons, there is a 12 person limit on each tour, and children must be at least eight years of age to participate.

Address 2601 Sheridan Road, Evanston, IL 60201, +1 (847) 328-6961, www.grossepointlighthouse.net // Getting there Purple Line to Central // Hours Daily dawn–dusk; see website for tour schedule // Ages 3+ (8+ for tours)

TIP: Visit the wildflower garden located at the rear of the lighthouse. Follow the garden path, which leads through the dune grasses and to the lakefront.

50_ HALIM TIME & GLASS MUSEUM

Where time keeps ticking beautifully by

If you could collect anything in the world, what would it be? Baseball cards? Bottlecaps? Stamps? Coins?

Ever since he was a little boy, Cameel Halim has been fascinated with time: "Timepieces. Since I was a little child, I was fascinated by how they were put together. The alarm clock in our house, I used to take it apart." He loved clocks so much that he began collecting them. He collected so many timepieces that the only way to display them all would be to open a museum. So that's just what he did.

The five-story Halim Time & Glass Museum houses over 1,100 timepieces from Halim's treasured collection. Eight rooms are dedicated to time pieces from around the world, including tower clocks, chronometers, automatons, pocket watches and tall case clocks, offering a unique glimpse into the history of timekeeping.

Four rooms house 70 stained-glass pieces of art, Halim's other hobby. Of note are the 30 masterpiece windows that showcase the masters of the American School of Stained Glass. The museum's third floor is capped with a stunning Tiffany ceiling and rooftop garden. Visitors are encouraged to touch the colorful glass panes, a rarity in the museum world.

Halim grew up in Egypt and emigrated to the United States in 1968 with only around $900 in savings, yet managed to become a successful property developer. He opened the museum in 2017 to thank the city of Chicago, which welcomed him when he was a poor immigrant with timely dreams.

Address 1560 Oak Avenue, Evanston, IL 60201, +1 (224) 714-5600, www.halimmuseum.org // Getting there Metra UP-N to Davis Street/ Evanston // Hours Tue–Sat 10am–5pm // Ages 3+

TIP: Sample authentic Liège waffles at Berry Pike Café!

51_ HAND-POWERED TRAINS

Loco for locomotives at Rehm Park

choo

If you've got a kid on your hands who is loco for locomotives, choo choo on over to Rehm Park in suburban Oak Park, where kids are invited to ride the rails. Since 1960, kids have been chugging along the track of this charming park. Only these trains aren't powered by steam or diesel: they're hand powered.

Hop aboard one of the many hand-powered engines and get cranking! Kids are welcome to blow off some steam and endlessly circle the 350-foot oval that winds around the playground via their personal, hand-cranked engine.

The trains here are similar to handcars, once an essential part of railroad operations from about 1850 to around 1910 and used for track construction and maintenance.

Tiny tots might need a push from Mom or Dad every now and then, but these train cars are easy to crank into motion. They're also free of charge. Remember to take turns as they are available on a first-come, first-served basis.

Reserve some time to play at the playground. A play structure at the center of the park features a climbable spider web and a tot-sized slide. Rehm Park itself is a wonderful spot to while away an afternoon. Pack a picnic and spread a blanket under a tree for a cheap play date with your train-loving little ones. It may be difficult to tear them away after all that fun, but a good night's sleep is guaranteed.

choo

choo

TIP: Visit Berwyn's Toys & Trains, a family-owned toy and hobby shop with model trains galore, located along historic Route 66 and housed in a former mid-century Chevy dealership.

Address 515 Garfield Street, Oak Park, IL 60304, +1 (708) 848-2929, pdop.org/parks-facilities/trains // Getting there Blue Line to Oak Park // Hours Daily dawn–dusk, see website for train schedule // Ages 3+

52_ THE HAPPY APPLE PIE SHOP

Made with love

The Happy Apple Pie Shop serves up some of the most delicious pies in Chicagoland, with three extra added ingredients: a dash of kindness, a sprinkle of community spirit, and a whole lotta love.

For owners Michelle Mascaro and Corynne Romine, their pie shop was a dream inspired by necessity. "As parents of a daughter who has an intellectual disability, we are painfully aware that there are far too few jobs available for people like her who want to work," they explain on their website. People with disabilities who do find work are often hidden away in sheltered workshops even today. So Mascaro and Romine decided to try doing things differently. Instead of keeping people with disabilities out of the public eye, they chose to create a blended workplace. So when you visit, you will meet people with and without developmental and intellectual disabilities, all working together to serve up tasty treats.

And that they do. The pies here may be even more delicious because they're made with team spirit. Patrons can watch the magic, as you can see directly into the kitchen from the sales counter. Though it's a small space, it is fully accessible, and there is room for everyone to stop, stay awhile, sip tea or coffee, and best of all, dig into a slice or two of pie.

You'll find three pies on the menu each week (always apple plus two other fruit pies). The savory quiches and pot pies make it possible to enjoy lunch and dessert on the spot.

Address 226 Harrison Street, Oak Park, IL 60304, +1 (708) 606-0037, www.happyapplepie.com, happyapplepiemakers@gmail.com // Getting there Blue Line to Austin // Hours Tue—Fri 10am—7pm, Sat & Sun 10am—4pm // Ages 3+

TIP: Galleries and studios in the Oak Park Arts District open their doors on the third Friday of each month with new exhibitions.

53_ HAROLD WASHINGTON SPEAKS

The slow walk towards greatness

At Chicago's DuSable Museum of African American History, a friendly face extends a robotic yet warm greeting to visitors at the center of the *Slow Walk to Greatness* exhibit.

"Hi, I am Harold Washington and welcome to my office," he graciously smiles behind the desk that he used while serving as a state representative in Springfield, Illinois. "This is the story of my time as a public servant, representing the good people of Illinois…"

This isn't *the* Harold Washington, lawyer, military veteran, and former Illinois state representative and senator, US congressman, and Chicago's first black mayor. But it's a pretty good likeness.

The DuSable team hired animatronic engineering firm Life Formations to create this robotic version of the city's beloved mayor. The animatronic Harold Washington comes alive with the touch of a button, sharing stories of his life, his service to our country, his mayoral campaign, and his biggest struggle ever: unifying the city. "Chicago is one city," he famously said. "We shall work as one people for our common good and our common goals."

Born in Chicago and raised in the Bronzeville neighborhood, the real Harold Washington was first elected as mayor in 1983. He's best remembered for emphasizing fairness and empowering neighborhoods during his service to the city. Sadly, Washington suffered a heart attack and died while in office on November 25, 1987. He was especially fond of the wild parakeets that live in Washington Park.

Address 740 E. 56th Place, Chicago, IL 60637, +1 (773) 947-0600, www.dusablemuseum.org // Getting there Green Line to Cottage Grove // Hours Tue–Sat 10am–5pm, Sun noon–5pm // Ages 3+

54_JUDY ISTOCK BUTTERFLY HAVEN'S FIRST FLIGHT

Winged beauty

Butterflies are the winged wonders of the natural world. Their four-stage life cycle transforms them from caterpillars to chrysalis to fluttering fantasies. It's rare to watch a newly-emerged butterfly spread its wings and take flight for the very first time, but at the Peggy Notebaert Nature Museum, guests can observe them in both their chrysalis and butterfly stages. Every day at 2pm, visitors gather in the Judy Istock Butterfly Haven to see them spread their wings and flutter into the lush, tropical Haven for the first time.

The Haven houses thousands of butterflies in its 2,700-square-foot greenhouse. You'll find them flapping around the pools of water, tropical flowers, and trees. Learn about the life cycle from caterpillar to chrysalis to butterfly before you enter, and then catch them in their chrysalides upon exit.

"With approximately 40 different species in the Haven at any given time, there's always a new favorite butterfly to discover!" shares John Bannon, marketing manager at the museum. "Fan-favorites are the blue morpho butterfly, a charismatic butterfly with iridescent blue wings. These butterflies are seen soaring through the Butterfly Haven in small groups, as if playing a game of 'follow the leader.' You'll find the rice paper butterfly, another large butterfly with translucent white wings and black markings resting on leaves soaking in the sun. The lacewing butterfly is also adored for its bright colors," says Bannon.

Address Peggy Notebaert Nature Museum, 2430 N. Cannon Drive, Chicago, IL 60614, +1 (773) 755-5100, www.naturemuseum.org // Getting there CTA bus 134, 143, 151 or 156 to Stockton & Arlington // Hours Butterfly Release daily 2pm, see website for museum hours // Ages 3+

TIP: Head to the always-free Lincoln Park Conservatory, located just across from the Notebaert Nature Center, and see if you can spot the mini ladybug trolley that zips around through the ferns of the display house.

55__ JUNIOR RANGER PROGRAM

Earn your badge at Pullman National Monument

Who doesn't dream of becoming a National Park Ranger, with their, broad-brimmed, high-crowned hats and unparalleled access to some of the most iconic historic and natural sites in the US?

At Chicago's Pullman National Monument, kids can now test their skills and take the oath to become an honorary Junior Ranger. If they pass the program successfully, they'll even receive an official badge. The activity-based program is conducted in almost all national parks, historic sites, and monuments, so kids can start their collection in Chicago and gather unique badges as they travel across the US in search of ranger adventures.

Pullman National Monument was designed as a planned utopia, where workers for the Palace Car Company, George Pullman's railcar manufacturing company, which opened at the beginning of the mid-19th century's railway boom in the US, could both live and work. As you tour the key landmarks and factories of this planned industrial community, you'll step back into a turbulent time in American history.

To become a Pullman National Monument Park Ranger, kids can pick up the official 10-page booklet at the Visitor Center. Depending on age, kids will need to complete a certain number of booklet activities as they tour the key landmarks and factories here. Activities include an outdoor scavenger hunt and an artifact BINGO game that will require searching for components of a Pullman railway car. Upon completion of the activities, check in with a park ranger and take the oath to become an official Junior Ranger.

Address 11141 S. Cottage Grove Avenue, Chicago, IL 60628, +1 (773) 468-9310, www.nps.gov/pull // Getting there Metra ME to 111th Street/ Pullman or Kensington/115th Street // Hours Tue 11am–3pm, Wed–Sun 9am–5pm // Ages 5+

TIP: Check out the children's book *A Long Hard Journey: The Story of the Pullman Porter* by Patricia C. McKissack and Fredrick L. McKissack from your local library. It tells the story of the Pullman porters, men hired to work on the railroads as porters on sleeping cars, many of whom were former slaves.

56_ KIPPER FAMILY ARCHAEOLOGY DISCOVERY CENTER

Dig for buried treasure like Indiana Jones

There's no better place in the city to embrace your inner Indiana Jones. Located on the picture-perfect University of Chicago campus in the Hyde Park neighborhood, the intimate Oriental Institute makes for the perfect spot to introduce kids to the joys of archaeology. Founded in 1919 by Professor James Henry Breasted, who could have inspired the swashbuckling character of Indiana Jones, the intriguing collection includes a colossal 40-ton, human-headed, winged bull, a 17-foot-tall statue of King Tutankhamun, and several fascinating mummies.

On the museum's lower level, an (artificial) ancient tel, or mound, gives kids the chance to dig for buried treasures the scientific way. Part of the Kipper Family Archaeology Discovery Center, the tel replicates the Middle Eastern mounds where actual Oriental Institute archaeologists dig. You'll have to register for a youth for family program – offered just about weekly throughout the year – to excavate this artifact-packed tel. Kids can expect to find oil lamps, jewelry, pottery shards, and human and animal figurines as they excavate the site using real tools and data-gathering techniques.

Before you head into the galleries, pick up a Kid Brochure from the front desk: it will explain the most precious objects in the collection and bring their importance and history down to a kid's level.

Be sure to check out the museum's collection of mummified small creatures, including a magnificent mummified lizard.

Address 1155 E. 58th Street, Chicago, IL 60637, +1 (773) 702-9514, oi.uchicago. edu/programs-events/youth-family-programs // Getting there Metra ME to University of Chicago/59th Street // Hours Tue–Sun 10am–5pm // Ages 5+

TIP: Play the Mummy game, an online game focused on how to prepare a mummy for burial, dreamt up by the Oriental Institute (oi-archive.uchicago.edu/OI/MUS/ED/mummy.html).

57 _ KITTEN NURSERY

Cuteness overload at the Windy Kitty

When Jenny Tiner was a little girl, she wasn't allowed to have a cat. Fast forward to adulthood, and Tiner, making up for lost time, has dozens of cats. That's because she's the "crazy for cats" lady behind the Windy Kitty, a cat café located on bustling North Avenue in Wicker Park.

Step inside this feline oasis for a bit of one-on-one time with some of the cutest creatures in town. The cats here are all rescued from the city shelter, trading in a grim future for this cat paradise. Patrons can purchase a drink or snack at the entrance and settle in for cuddles. Plenty of toys, such as feather wands, are on hand if you care to play a game of cat and mouse. But if it's cuteness overload you're after, the kitten nursery at the rear of the café is where playful kittens reign.

Why a kitten nursery?

"It was a dream of mine to have a kitten nursery be a part of the Windy Kitty since before I opened!" explained Tiner. When orphaned kittens come to city shelters, they are extremely vulnerable if they are still nursing because shelters often simply don't have the time and resources to feed them and care for them overnight. Tiner's idea was to make The Windy Kitty a safe haven and a place for them give them a chance at a wonderful life.

Best of all, all kittens are available for adoption, so if your kid falls in love with a fluffy one, you can start the application process on the spot.

"A lot of cat cafés won't allow kids," said Tiner. "But I want to make it easier for families to find a cat that fits their family. I love to see a positive relationship start early."

TIP: Take some time to visit nearby historic Wicker Park, where a large children's playground with an interactive water spray feature, ornamental community gardens, and a historic fountain await.

Address 1746 W. North Avenue, Chicago, IL 60622, www.windykittychicago.com, meow@windykittychicago.com // Getting there Blue Line to Damen // Hours Wed–Sat 10am–1pm & 3–7pm, Sun noon–6pm // Ages 10+

58_ LABYRINTH AT FOURTH PRESBY- TERIAN CHURCH

It's a-maze-ing

Daedalus was a craftsman so skillful that King Minos asked him to build his grand palace and also an elaborate labyrinth to confuse and trap the dastardly Minotaur, a half-man-half-bull of a beast. But then King Minos turned on Daedalus, jailing him in his labyrinth together with his son Icarus. The brilliant Daedalus had so carefully crafted the labyrinth that even he couldn't figure out how to make an escape.

Since ancient times, labyrinths have been made for meditation, a way to walk your way into contemplation. The labyrinth at gothic revival Fourth Presbyterian Church, located in its Buchanan Chapel, is made of limestone tiles and is a modified version of the medieval labyrinth in the Gothic Chartres Cathedral in France. It takes about 20 minutes to walk. Follow the labyrinth's seven circuits round and round until you're truly spirited... and a tad dizzy.

As the church's website explains, however, it's not exactly a maze (though if you do find yourself lost within its circuits, you can always build a pair of wings, as did Daedalus, who also built a pair for his son, with which they flew out of the labyrinth of Knossos.) "One does not have to think about finding the right way or worry about getting lost... It is also a place of presence; which can help us listen to inner wisdom and gain new understandings. The labyrinth symbolizes life's journey and offers us time to think about our path.

Address 126 E. Chestnut Street, Chicago, IL 60611, +1 (312) 787-4570, www.fourthchurch.org // Getting there Red Line to Chicago // Hours See website for hours and availability // Ages 3+

TIP: The cornerstone inscription at Holy Name Cathedral, the seat of the Catholic Archdiocese of Chicago, bears bullet marks from the murder of gangster Hymie Weiss, who was killed across the street on October 11, 1926.

59_ LEANING TOWER OF NILES

La dolce vita... in Chicagoland

You don't have to travel all the way to Italy to see the leaning tower of Pisa. Niles, which directly borders Chicago's far northwest side, is home to a half-size replica of the famed *Torre Pendente di Pisa*.

The 183-foot-tall Pisa original, built in 1372, wasn't always leaning. It began to tilt soon after construction, the iconic result of an inadequate foundation. Over the years, efforts to bring the tower to a fully upright stance failed, though today its signature tilt is stabilized at 3.99 degrees.

In 1934, industrialist Robert Ilg built a leaning tower of his very own in Niles. It was just one part of a vast recreational complex for the employees of Ilg Hot Air Electric Ventilating Company, built to store water for the once on-site swimming pools. The 94-foot tower honors scientist Galileo Galilei, who tested his theory of gravity by dropping objects from the original tower in Pisa, with a plaque at its base.

Listen for the bronze bells in the tower, three of which were cast in 17th- and 18th-century Italy. They were recently restored and are now tolling once again.

The surrounding *piazza* features four fountains, as well as a 30-foot reflecting pool, and makes for the perfect picnic spot, not unlike Pisa's Piazza del Duomo.

Harness the power of forced perspective and snap a selfie standing before the tower so that it appears as if you're holding it up with your own mighty muscle power.

TIP: Grab a Chicago Deep Dish Pizza with a caramelized crust from Pequod's Pizza and enjoy a picnic in the piazza.

Address 6300 W. Touhy Avenue, Niles, IL 60714 // **Getting there** Blue Line to Cumberland, then CTA bus 290 to Touhy & Mobile Avenue // **Hours** Mon – Fri 5am – 10pm, Sat 5am – 7pm, Sun 6am – 5pm // **Ages** 3+

60__LILACIA PARK

Surround yourself with beauty

Every spring, as early as the second week of May through mid-June, the suburban town of Lombard blooms with purple plumes. Sweet perfume fills the air. Residents flock to Lilacia Park, where an 8.5-acre garden is filled with lilacs, the flowers of our most fragrant dreams and memories.

Busbecquis, the ambassador of the Imperial Hapsburgs to the Turkish Sultan, first cultivated lilacs and then brought them out into the greater world to Vienna. From Imperial Austria, the *Syringa vulgaris* spread to France and eventually... suburban Lombard.

Civil War veteran Colonel William Plum and his wife Helen Maria Williams Plum settled in Babcock's Grove, the former name of Lombard, in the late 1860s, building an estate that would eventually come to be known as Lilacia upon their return from a grand European tour, which included a visit to the famous gardens of Victor Lemoine in Nancy, France. Lemoine's nursery was renowned for developing French lilacs with extremely fragrant double blossoms, and the Plums purchased two lilacs: *Syringa vulgaris* 'Mme Casimir Périer,' a double white, and *Syringa vulgaris* 'Michel Buchner,' a double lilac color, the two cultivars that grew into the grand, lilac-filled garden of today.

Upon their deaths, the Plums gifted their gardens to the people of Lombard as a public park. Famous landscape architect Jens Jensen was commissioned to design beloved Lilacia Park.

Kids will love making their way through the glorious, scented maze of over 700 lilacs and 25,000 tulips. For the first two weeks of May, the park plays host to Lilac Time, a two-week celebration that offers kid-friendly crafts, concerts, tours and other floral festivities.

Address 150 S. Park Avenue, Lombard, IL 60148, +1 (630) 620-7322, www.lombardlilactime.com // Getting there Metra UP-W to Lombard, IL // Hours Daily dawn–dusk // Ages 3+

TIP: Visit the Enchanted Castle with indoor go-karts, laser tag, bumper cars, rides, mini-bowling, miniature golf, karaoke, singing dragons, and a two-story playland.

61_ LOGAN BOULEVARD SKATE PARK

The gnarliest park on the North Side

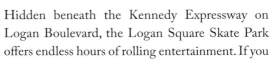

Hidden beneath the Kennedy Expressway on Logan Boulevard, the Logan Square Skate Park offers endless hours of rolling entertainment. If you have a kid who's already an advanced boarder, or a beginner looking to test their skills, this edgy, 1.29-acre skate park promises to challenge both with its modular obstacles and ramps.

Once upon a time, this space was dark and underused. Today, it's well-lit and filled with a colorful community of characters. As the city's only covered skatepark, rain or shine this space is always buzzing with the whirring sound of skateboards. Installation artist and sculptor Lucy Slivinski used found tail pipes, hubcaps, and colorful lenses from old traffic signals to create the Silversurf Gate that surrounds the park; its concrete pillars are festooned with graffiti art.

Though the park is shared by skateboarders and BMX bicyclists alike, you'll mostly find skateboarders of all ages honing their latest tricks. Smaller kids might want to work on their balance and agility on a scooter before setting off on a skateboard.

Obstacles include a bowl corner with a ledge to launch off or rest upon, a variety of smaller ramps, handrails for grinding and sliding, and a funbox, a box-shaped structure with a flat top and ramps on the sides. A picnic table and a bench are made for skating tricks, but you can also use them to rest your weary bones.

TIP: Fuel up on BBQ classics on the porch or patio at Fat Willy's Rib Shack, located on a side street a block or so past the northern edge of the bridge.

Address 2430 W. Logan Boulevard,
Chicago, IL 60647, +1 (312) 742-7552,
www.chicagoparkdistrict.com // Getting
there Blue Line to Western, then CTA
bus 49 to Western & Logan/Jones //
Hours Daily 6am–11pm // Ages 3+

62_MAGGIE DALEY PLAY GARDEN

The coolest park in the city

At the southeast section of Maggie Daley Park, beyond the skating ribbon, rock-climbing walls, picnic groves, and tennis courts, a pirate's ship, an enchanted forest, a watering hole, an imaginary harbor, and a moon crater invite kids 12 and under to jump, slide, swing, leap, hide, seek, and perhaps most importantly, imagine. The three-acre Play Garden, the first of its kind in Chicago, is by far *the* coolest park in the city.

Stroll the Enchanted Forest's winding pathways, lined with upside-down trees, towards the Turning Stone, a giant, upright stone that rotates on its vertical axis, so that even a small child can move it with a bit of effort. Board the pirate ship, which 'floats' in the middle of 'the sea,' waiting patiently for little buccaneers to climb its ladders and catch fish in its nets. With a little help from the Lighthouse Tower's kid-powered beacon, talking tubes, periscopes, and spiral exit slide, pirate kids can safely steer their ship through the treacherous waves.

Little ones ages 2–5 will want to cool off at the Watering Hole, an animal-themed playground with water spray features perfect for hot summer days. The harbor is another spot for the preschool set, with its covered central marina and three full-sized play boats.

Older kids will want to make a beeline to the crater, where spiral slides, rail slides, and slides that emerge from a Play Pyramid offer hours of thrills. These are the fastest slides in the city, so prepare for a grand *whoosh* straight down towards the (rubberized) ground.

Address 337 E. Randolph Street, Chicago, IL 60601, +1 (312) 552-3000, www.chicagoparkdistrict.com/parks // Getting there Brown, Green, Orange, Pink, or Purple Line to State/Lake // Hours Daily 6am–11pm // Ages 3+

TIP: Millennium Park's Harris Theater for Music and Dance plays host to the Exelon Family Series of hour-long, kid-friendly, world-class performances on Saturdays at 2pm. No shushing allowed! Tickets cost less than a trip to the movie theater and are available online.

63_MARIO'S ITALIAN LEMONADE

Summertime's classic curbside treat

yes

Mario DiPaolo was a rambunctious little kindergartener. He was so rambunctious his parents decided to put his energy to work: in 1954, they bought a shaved ice maker and parked it in front of their little storefront in the heart of Chicago's Little Italy, where Mario happily hand-cranked old-fashioned lemonade ices by the dozen, selling them at two cents a cup. When Mario's Italian Lemonade re-opens every year in May, summertime in Chicago can officially commence.

Mario's Italian lemonade is an Americanized take on the traditional Italian *granita*, a slushy, shaved ice treat flavored with real ultra-pureed fruits. You'll find a rainbow of fruity flavors – more than a dozen are on the daily rotating menu. But lemon remains the all-time favorite, and minuscule lemon rinds dot every icy concoction.

Avoid a terrible case of brain freeze by slurping the deliciousness with a spoon. You'll also find a number of Italian savory snacks, such as lupini beans, dried chickpeas, and roasted nuts, all of which are salty enough to pair perfectly with the icy sweetness.

There is no seating at this red, white, and green painted stand, but on a hot summer's night, sitting on the nearby curb with family and friends new and old is the best way to enjoy this tart and sugary taste of Taylor Street.

> TIP: Across from the Conte di Savoia grocery store, two public bocce courts welcome players young and old to give the ancient Roman ball-tossing game a try.

"SPECIAL"

FRUIT COCKTAIL

ITALIAN LEMONADE

TUTTi FRuTTi

Address 1066 W. Taylor Street, Chicago, IL 60607 // Getting there Blue Line to UIC-Halsted // Hours May–Sep, daily 11am–midnight // Ages 3+

64_ MCDONALD'S GLOBAL MENU RESTAURANT AT HAMBURGER U.

Trade your Big Mac for a Big McAloo Tikki

It's one of the top universities in the US, even harder to get into than Harvard and boasting more than 80,000 graduates since it was established in 1961. But the only degree you can obtain at this institution of higher learning is a bachelor's in Hamburgerology. McDonald's flagship Hamburger University, which relocated in 2018 to downtown Chicago on the site of Oprah Winfrey's former Harpo Studios, is where McDonald's employees and future leaders learn the ropes of building the perfect burger and much, much more.

While the university is only open to select students, the ground floor is home to a one-of-a-kind McDonald's restaurant that welcomes kids with adventurous palates with a rotating menu of favorites from McD's around the globe. Menu items include *poutine* from Canada, Mozza Salad from France, Wasabi Shake Shake Fries from Hong Kong, and the tasty, vegan McAloo Tikki from India among the many international treats you'll want to try. Save room for dessert: the Baci McFlurry from Italy and the McFlurry Prestígio from Brazil are highly recommended. Check out the enormous, ever-changing wall map with Golden Arches that illuminate when an item from a specific country is featured on the menu.

At more than 6,000 square feet with sleek seating and streetside views of Randolph Street, Chicago's bustling foodie central, this Experience of the Future (EOTF) restaurant is the most modern McD's you'll ever encounter.

Address 1035 W. Randolph, Chicago, IL 60607, +1 (312) 291-9224, www.facebook.com/mcdonaldsheadquarters // Getting there Green or Pink Line to Morgan // Hours Daily 6am–10pm // Ages 3+

TIP: Nearby, Mary Bartelme Park is home to a play area, a modern fountain plaza with misting spray features, and a climbable hill with city vistas.

65_ METHOD SOAP FACTORY

See how it's made

Adam Lowry dreamed of finding green cleaners that actually worked and smelled good. Eric Ryan wondered why cleaning products are so poorly designed. Together, these two childhood friends birthed a brilliant idea: Method, a line of sustainable soaps made with non-toxic ingredients "that clean like heck and smell like heaven."

Established in 2001, when the duo landed their first sale of four cleaning sprays to a small California grocery store, Method now stands as one of the top eco-conscious companies in the world. Take a tour of their colorful Pullman-based factory, and you'll see the soapmaking process in action. You'll also learn how pioneers like Method are working to find solutions to climate change.

First you'll need to don a stylish hairnet, safety glasses, and vest. Kids will be mesmerized by the carefully orchestrated precision of the manufacturing process and the thousands of interesting-shaped bottles marching down the assembly line.

But it's Method's green initiatives that truly amaze.

The certified LEED Platinum factory is located on 22 acres of land, much of which is a wildlife and natural habitat. A 230-foot wind turbine works the opposite of a fan, using wind to make electricity. Three 35 x 35-foot solar tracking trees in the parking lot also gather energy. Method's plastic bottles are also made on-site out of recycled materials. Even the rooftop is green: it's covered with 75,000 square feet of growing greens that will eventually make their way into salads across the city.

Address 720 E. 111th Street, Chicago, IL 60628, +1 (866) 963-8463, www.methodhome.com // Getting there Metra ME to 111th Street/Pullman // Hours Group tours with advance reservations // Ages 3+

TIP: Stock up on organic fruits and veggies at the Pullman Farmers' Market on Wednesdays from June through October, 7am to 1pm.

66_MIDNIGHT CIRCUS

Under the little big top in the parks

At the end of every August, royal purple and lavender-striped 'little big tops' take over parks across the city when the Midnight Circus comes to town for its annual, nine-week tour de fun and excitement for all ages. Acrobats, aerialists, contortionists, clowns, tightrope walkers, jugglers, and even comedic canines bring their fantastical arts straight to the heart of the community via intimate, two-hour performances that allow audiences to get up-close to the onstage action. Touching down in a new neighborhood every week, this affordable, accessible, spirited circus contributes all proceeds raised to fund improvements in parks throughout the City of Chicago.

Jeff and Julie Jenkins founded the circus in 2007 after a trip to Europe led them to fall in love will small-scale performances in local piazzas. Today it's a family affair: their kids Maxwell and Samantha are in on the act, too. Their beloved Midnight Circus has now raised over a million dollars in park enhancements.

Volunteers are at the heart of this circus. Community members sell the tickets, pop the popcorn, and usher over 15,000 audience members to their seats at little big tops throughout the city each year.

Animal welfare is another core value of the Midnight Circus, and the cast always includes incredible rescue 'bully breed' dog acrobats that have overcome the odds to become much adored performers and ambassadors.

The playful pitbulls work to encourage families to adopt – not shop – for their next pet.

> **TIP:** PAWS, Chicago's Youth Volunteer Program, enables children ages 12 through 17 to volunteer, together with a parent or legal guardian, to help homeless pets.

Address Various locations,
www.midnightcircus.net,
+1 (312) 343-4955,
tickets@midnightcircus.net //
Getting there See website
for event locations // Hours
Aug–Oct, see website for
shows and schedule // Ages 3+

67_ MITSUWA MARKETPLACE

Switch up your usual grocery shopping routine

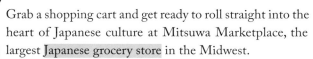

Grab a shopping cart and get ready to roll straight into the heart of Japanese culture at Mitsuwa Marketplace, the largest Japanese grocery store in the Midwest.

Mitsuwa is so much more than your standard supermarket. It's as close as you'll get to the sights, sounds, and flavors of the Land of the Rising Sun without having to hop on an airplane at nearby O'Hare.

Switch up your usual grocery shopping routine and drag your kids here instead. They'll feel as if they've stepped foot in another country, though no doubt they'll recognize some of the characters scattered about – Pikachu, Hello Kitty, Totoro, and other beloved anime friends all make appearances on everything from ramen noodle packages to colorful candies to pop bottles.

You'll find everything you need from your weekly shopping list – with a Japanese twist. Head to the snack aisle for a new take on treats, such as seaweed crackers, scallop-flavored chips, and the elusive green tea KitKat candy bars. Stock up on soda in flavors like lychee, corn, and banana. The fruit and veg aisle is home to persimmons, yuzu, lotus root, and more colorful vitamin-packed goodies. The in-store bakery's shelves are packed with colorful desserts, including turtle-shaped buns filled with custard and red bean-dotted Danishes. The bookstore features bilingual comics, colorful stationery goods, and character collectibles, all irresistibly attractive to kawaii-loving kids.

Save time for the bustling food court, which offers some of the best and most affordable Japanese food in the area, including tempura delights, sushi, and ramen noodles, an international kids' favorite.

TIP: Grab some Japanese treats to go and enjoy a picnic and catch-and-release fishing at Lake Arlington.

Address 100 E. Algonquin Road, IL
Arlington Heights, +1 (847) 956-6699,
www.mitsuwa.com/ch // Getting there
Blue Line to Rosemont, then CTA bus
606 to Algonquin Road & Tonne Drive //
Hours Daily 9am – 9pm // Ages 3+

68__MOLD-A-RAMA

Vintage souvenirs, molded on the spot

Mold-A-Rama machines have been churning out their colorful signature molded plastic souvenir figurines at Chicago-area museums and zoos since the early 1960s. Ask any older Chicagoan if they remember 'the smell,' and chances are they'll recall with keen nostalgia the warm, plastic fragrance of a Mold-A-Rama figurine, fresh from the machine. You can still find these vintage machines hidden in the quieter corners and corridors of local museums and zoos.

The glass-topped plastic-injection Mold-A-Rama vending machines were created in Chicago and manufactured by Automatic Retailers of America, later known as Aramark, in 1962. Though the machines quickly spread across the country, many fell into disrepair. But you'll still find many machines alive and well in the Chicagoland area.

Place a few coins in the slot and in less than a minute, you can watch as the machine pumps plastic into a two-piece mold, hollows it out, and then cools it before depositing your colorful figurine into a tray, still warm to the touch.

Though you'll find the vintage machines at many cultural sites, the most sought-after Mold-A-Rama figurines include the green hippo, made in a machine located at the west end of the Pachyderm building at Brookfield Zoo (8400 W. 31st Street, Brookfield, IL, 60513); the orange stegosaurus and green brontosaurus, located in the basement of the Field Museum (1400 S. Lake Shore Drive); and the blue Chicago skyline, made in a machine located in the main gift shop at Willis Tower (233 S. Wacker Drive).

Make a point of seeking out all the Mold-A-Rama machines for a collection of timeless souvenirs molded into life before your very eyes.

> TIP: Visit Ka-Pow Collectibles for a museum-worthy selection of vintage and unusual collectible toys.

Address Various locations, www.mold-a-rama.com //
Getting there See website for location addresses //
Hours Vary by location //Ages 3+

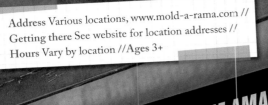

69_ MOLLY'S CUPCAKES

Stay and swing awhile

Cupcakes, glorious cupcakes. At Molly's Cupcakes, these perfectly kid-sized cakes are baked in small batches throughout the day, "with only the finest and freshest ingredients in the city."

Prepare to find your sweet cupcake soul mate. The center-filled cupcakes are the stars and come in several flavors, including cake batter, crème brûlée, peanut butter Nutella, and peach cobbler. The classic cupcakes - chocolate, vanilla, carrot, red velvet, and banana - are quite simply exquisite. Each season brings new flavors to the colorful display case.

You can also create your very own cupcake! Pick a cake flavor, choose a frosting, and then choose from a number of tasty toppings, and a baker will make it right in front of you. Because this is a place to overindulge, make a beeline for the delightful Sprinkle Station, where you can further personalize your cupcake with a selection of colorful confetti.

John Nicolaides, the founder of Molly's Cupcakes, named his adorable shop after his third-grade teacher. "Whenever one of us had a birthday, she would bake us cupcakes. I still remember how good they were." So it's no surprise that Molly's Cupcakes has a schoolyard feel, complete with playground equipment – swings replace stools at the cozy bar, inviting kids and kids at heart to stay and swing awhile. Plus cupcakes just taste better when eaten while swinging.

In honor of the much-loved school teacher, a portion of the profits here are donated directly to neighborhood schools. So every time you bite into a sweet cupcake, you are investing in the people and schools that will create the brightest future for the city.

Address 2536 N. Clark Street, Chicago, IL 60614, +1 (773) 883-7220, www.mollyscupcakes.com, info@mollyscupcakes.com // Getting there CTA bus 36 to Clark/Deming // Hours Mon noon–10pm, Tue–Sat 8am–10pm, Sun 9am–10pm // Ages 3+

TIP: Adjacent to Molly's Cupcakes, Belmont Flower Market specializes in baby bonsai trees and lucky bamboo shoots.

70_MONEY MUSEUM

Show me the money!

What would you do if you came across a briefcase stuffed with one million dollars?

At the Money Museum, located on the first floor of the Federal Reserve Bank of Chicago, you're bound to encounter the tempting briefcase, brimming with shiny, fresh $100 bills. While you can't take it with you – if only! – you can pose for a picture standing beside it and dream of all the things you'd do with the easy cash. And don't worry, you'll be gifted a little bag of money if you ask one of the museum docents, but it will be perfectly shredded and useless.

The Federal Reserve Bank of Chicago is one of 12 regional reserve banks that make up our nation's central bank. Its in-house Money Museum is dedicated to telling the story of the almighty US dollar.

From a preserved pine tree shilling from colonial America, to notes from the US Civil War, to contemporary cash, you'll find plenty of money to go around. Games and simulations give kids the chance to save the economy via monetary policy decision-making. Or they can step into the shoes of a Secret Service agent to detect counterfeit bills. And they can help banks run safely from the perspective of a bank manager.

You won't need to spend a dime at this small but fascinating museum, as admission is always free. This is the Chicago Fed, however, so be ready to show photo identification, walk through a metal detector, and have your bags X-rayed before entering.

Address 230 S. LaSalle Street, Chicago, IL 60604, +1 (312) 322-2400, www.chicagofed.org/education/money-museum/index // Getting there Brown, Purple, Pink, or Orange Line to Quincy // Hours Mon–Fri 8:30am–5pm // Ages 3+

TIP: This portion of LaSalle Street, the so-called LaSalle Canyon, was used as the backdrop for the 2005 film *Batman Begins* and its sequel, *The Dark Knight*.

71_ N. W. HARRIS LEARNING COLLECTION

Bring the museum home with you

It's one thing to visit the museum. But what if the museum could come home with you?

Imagine heading into the Field Museum and taking a taxidermied eel, the diorama of a gold mine, replicas of Stone Age tools, a balafon, or the model of an ancient Egyptian tomb back home?

Thanks to the N. W. Harris Learning Collection at the Field Museum, you can take your pick from over 400 cases and 70 different Experience Boxes (hands-on kits), each packed with museum-worthy goodies that are just waiting to be explored by curious kids. The categories include People, Animals, Plants, and Fossils/Rocks/Minerals.

These cases used to travel to public schools around the city, and though the primary audience is teachers, anyone can rent a case for up to four weeks. You do need to purchase a membership package, which starts at $35 for five rentals. You can also purchase a one-item membership package for $10 if you want to try the experience first.

Order the exact case that piques your interest online, then head to the museum to pick it up at the Ground Level near the West Entrance. N. W. Harris Learning Collection members can park along the curb with their flashers on and enter The Field Museum via the West Door. Take advantage of the full month-long period for examining, researching, and learning about the objects in every case you bring to your new, in-home museum.

Address Field Museum, 1400 S. Lake Shore Drive, Chicago, IL 60605, +1 (312) 922-9410, harris.fieldmuseum.org, harris@fieldmuseum.org // Getting there CTA bus 146 to Soldier Field & Field Museum // Hours Tue & Wed 3–7pm, Sat 9am–5pm // Ages 3+

TIP: Create your own in-home learning zone with supplies from the Chicago Teacher Store, where you'll find plenty of science and history-related educational tools and games.

72_NICHOLS TOWER

The original Sears (a.k.a. Willis) Tower

In 1973, the 110-story, 1,450-foot-tall Sears Tower popped up in the Chicago skyline, towering far above its fellow skyscrapers. Built by the now-bankrupt Sears, Roebuck & Co., one of the largest retailers in the world at the time of its construction, it boasted the title of 'Tallest Building in the World.' Few Chicagoans know that it was preceded by a humbler but no less extraordinary tower, the 14-story Nichols Tower in North Lawndale, also built by Sears, Roebuck & Co. in 1906.

Today, the Neo-Classical warehouse tower stands alone, though it originally was built as the crown centerpiece of the vast Sears, Roebuck & Co. complex, which included the Sears Catalog Facility, now razed but once the largest wood-frame structure in the world.

While the tower housed primarily management offices, it also broadcasted WLS-AM – World's Largest Store radio, still booming out news and talk shows on the radio waves today from its 11th floor. As the company lost its footing, the zone was largely demolished. In 1988, Sears, Roebuck & Co. stepped in again to repurpose the 55-acre site. Along the way, it acquired a new name: Homan Square.

Today, Nichols Tower stands as a community beacon of hope, housing the Lawndale Business Renaissance Association, the North Lawndale Employment Network, a branch of the School of the Art Institute of Chicago, and Sweet Beginnings, a program that trains formerly incarcerated locals in the art of beekeeping. Don't miss a visit to the top floors, where you'll be greeted by sweeping views of the city.

TIP: The in-tower Lunchbox Cafe is the perfect place to refresh and re-energize with sandwiches, salads, snacks, baked goods, and drinks.

Address 906 S. Homan Avenue, Chicago, IL 60624, +1 (773) 265-5001, www.homansquare.org, info@homansquare.com // **Getting there** Blue Line to Kedzie-Homan // **Hours** Daily 9am–6pm // **Ages** 3+

73 _ NIGHT AT THE MUSEUM, AQUARIUM, OR ZOO

Sleep with the fishes, T. rex, or live elephants.

Have you ever wanted to snooze with Sue the T. rex? Explore a mummy-filled gallery... by flashlight? Sleep with the fishes – literally? So many beloved Chicago institutions offer overnights for families, making for an exciting city adventure like no other.

The Field Museum hosts Dozin' with the Dinos on select evenings throughout the year. You'll spend the night at the museum and go exploring after dark to view ancient Egyptian culture by flashlight or sneak around the savanna where giraffes and lions lurk. Sleep alongside dinosaurs - if you dare close your eyes.

Spend the night at the Museum of Science and Industry's Snoozeum, and you can set off on a scavenger hunt, build your own science toys, or make a magical slime concoction. Go to sleep next to a giant bating heart or a whirling tornado, or close your eyes beside a real submarine.

Settle in for the night with the starfish, eels, squid, dolphins, and sharks at the Shedd Aquarium's Asleep with the Fishes overnight stay. Offered on several nights throughout the year, this program lets you get up close to all the fishes you love, play games, and fall asleep among the sea creatures.

Campout at the Lincoln Park Zoo is an sleepover event that takes place at night, when many animals are more active. Pitch your own campsite and enjoy visits with the animals, fun activities, and a campfire with s'mores.

TIP: Pick up all the camping gear you need, including lanterns, canteens, and sleeping bags, at Army Navy Surplus USA.

Address Field Museum: www.fieldmuseum.org;
Museum of Science and Industry: www.msichicago.org;
Shedd Aquarium: www.sheddaquarium.org; Lincoln
Park Zoo: lpzoo.org // Getting there See websites
for addresses // Hours Vary by location and event //
Ages Science Snoozeum 6–12, others 5–12

74_ NOAH'S PLAYGROUND FOR EVERYONE

Everyone deserves to have fun

Noah Aaron Cutter was born in 2003 with neurological anomalies that made it difficult for him to enjoy a visit to the playground. When he passed away at the tender age of two, his parents Julie and David, along with his sister Ali, set off on a mission to build a playground in his memory, a playground where every child would feel welcome. They gathered the advice of special educators and therapists. In 2008, they inaugurated Noah's Playground on Evanston's lakefront.

Got a disability? No problem! This playground's amenities include accessible parking with a ramp system that will take you straight to the brightly colored structures. A tactile map showcases the layout. Interactive bells offer a chance to play with sound. An elevated sandbox makes it easy to pull up a wheelchair and get straight to building castles. The swings offer more comfort and support, so everyone can try to touch the clouds with their toes. Hop into the car or airplane structures and zip away faster than the imaginary speed of lightning. The entire playground is beautifully landscaped with trees ready to offer shade and a picture-perfect view of Lake Michigan.

Both special needs and non-special needs children and their families can count on quieter nooks, as well as accessible bathrooms and two-tiered drinking fountains. It's a great place to while away an afternoon complete with a picnic.

A small placard shares a memory of the little boy who inspired the playground: *Noah brought joy and light into the lives of everyone he met.*

Address 1431 Judson Avenue, Evanston, IL 60201 // Getting there Purple Line to Central // Hours Daily 8am–9pm // Ages 3+

75_NORTH PARK NATURE VILLAGE LOOP

Take a hike

Today, the North Park Nature Village, a 46-acre nature preserve where you can catch a breath of fresh air in the middle of the city, is one of the best places in the city to take a hike. Built in 1915, however, this spot was once the city's central tuberculosis sanitarium, the largest in the country with 650 beds, saving the lives of countless people, a witness to the devastation of this deadly, highly contagious disease.

Pass through the Nature Center, making sure to visit the Discovery Room, a hands-on table of natural objects, and the other interactive exhibits, and head out the back door, where the start of the loop hiking trail awaits. At a slow pace, it takes about an hour to hike the entire loop, making this a great hike for little legs.

The best part of this trail is that it provides a beautiful snapshot of Illinois' diverse flora and fauna, carrying hikers through wetlands, tallgrass prairie land, forests, and even oak savanna. It's easy to note the change in ecosystems as you follow the trail; interpretive signage geared towards children offers further insights.

Plan on encountering plenty of creatures along the trail: wood ducks, geese, garden snakes, painted turtles, deer, raccoons, foxes, bullfrogs, kingfishers, crayfish, and great blue herons all call this corner of the city home. Step atop the observational area, raised up from the Main Loop trail about half way along the wetlands, where you'll have a better view of the stunning native landscape.

Address 5801 N. Pulaski Road, Chicago, IL 60646, +1 (312) 744-5472, www.chicagoparkdistrict.com/parks/North-Park-Village-Nature-Center // Getting there Blue Line to Irving Park, then CTA bus 53 to Pulaski & Ardmore // Hours Daily 6am–11pm // Ages 3+

TIP: The annual Winter Solstice Festival, hosted every December, celebrates the longest night of the year with a giant bonfire, roasted chestnuts, hot cocoa, and naturalist-led activities, including a chance to meet some of the center's resident critters.

76_THE ORACLE
OF BRONZEVILLE

Gwendolyn Brooks' outdoor office

Gwendolyn Brooks brought both the beauty and hard reality of African-American life on the South Side to the forefront through her prolific writing career. She captured the vitality of her neighborhood, Bronzeville, the cultural hub of Black America, through her words. Though she was born in Topeka, Kansas on June 7, 1917, Brooks was raised in Chicago and lived here from the age of two until her death on December 3, 2000. Her parents encouraged her poetry writing, and she was submitting her poems to publications as a teen. A prolific writer, she was the author of more than 20 books of poetry, including *Children Coming Home; Annie Allen,* for which she received the Pulitzer Prize; and *A Street in Bronzeville.* She also wrote a novel, *Maud Martha* and a memoir, *Report from Part One: An Autobiography.* In 1968 she was named poet laureate for the State of Illinois, and in 1985, she was the first black woman appointed as consultant in poetry to the Library of Congress, a post now known as the United States Poet Laureate.

This new park, inaugurated in 2018 and located less than one mile from her childhood home at 4332 South Champlain, celebrates Brooks, the 'Oracle of Bronzeville,' and includes a sculpted bust of Brooks and her 'outdoor office,' which is a porch modeled after her childhood writing spot. There is a stepping stone path etched with quotations from *Annie Allen*, and a stone circle. Play structures with swings and slides, as well as a water splash and play area, make this a fun park for kids of all ages, with an added literary and history bonus.

Address 4532 S. Greenwood Avenue, Chicago, IL 60653 // Getting there Metra ME to 47th Street (Kenwood) // Hours Daily dawn–dusk // Ages 3+

TIP: Pick up a copy of *Bronzeville Boys and Girls,* Gwendolyn Brooks' 1956 collection of poems for and about children in the surrounding neighborhood and read a few poems together on the stepping stones.

Gwendolyn Brooks: The Oracle of Bronzeville
June 7, 1917 - December 3, 2000
Margot McMahon

Pulitzer Prize in Poetry (1950)
American Academy of Arts and Letters (1976)
Poet Laureate of the United States (1985)
National Women's Hall of Fame (1988)
Robert Frost Medal (1989)
National Endowment for the Humanities,
Jefferson Lecturer (1994)
National Medal of Arts (1995)
Illinois Poet Laureate (1968 - 2000)
Chicago Literary Hall of Fame (2010)

77_ORIGINAL RAINBOW CONE

Feed your inner unicorn

Joseph Sapp was an orphan and grew up on a work farm in the early 1900s. Though he often saved up his hard-earned pennies for a simple vanilla ice cream cone, he dreamed of a cone that featured every flavor under the rainbow. In his late teens, he became a Buick mechanic and once again saved up his hard-earned money, dollars this time, with ice cream in mind. In 1926, his technicolor dream came true when he opened Original Rainbow together with wife Katherine.

An original rainbow cone is the official treat of hot summer nights in the city. Driving down Western Avenue on Chicago's South Side neighborhood of Beverly, you'll know you've arrived when you spot the giant ice cream cone that stands as a beacon on the rooftop of this cotton candy pink ice cream palace. On summer nights, it's always an ice cream party at Original Rainbow Cone. There is no seating in the shop, so patrons head to the parking lot, which is lit up with colorful strings of light. Some people even bring lawn chairs and make an evening of it.

Rainbow cones are the giants of the ice cream world, stacked with horizontal layers of chocolate, strawberry, Palmer House (walnut, cherry, and French vanilla), pistachio, and orange sherbet. Melded together in-cone, the flavors are at once distinguishable while also creating an entirely new flavor. It all depends upon how you decide to lick your rainbow cone: concentrating on one layer at a time or gathering as many of the five flavors on your tongue as you can.

Address 9233 S. Western Avenue, Chicago, IL 60643, +1 (773) 238-7075, www.rainbowcone.com // Getting there Red Line to 95th/Dan Ryan, then CTA bus 95 to Western & 92nd Place // Hours Daily, see website for seasonal hours // Ages 3+

78_OZ PARK

Over the rainbow

It all started with a bedtime story after a blustery day. In the 1890s, L. Frank Baum, a reporter for the *Chicago Evening Post*, wove a nighttime tale for his very own kids. A cyclone whirls a young farm girl and her little dog up and away and into a land inhabited by merry Munchkins, winged monkeys, a wicked witch, and a charlatan ruler. He named his invented land Oz after he glimpsed upon his file cabinet labeled 'O–Z.' In 1939, Baum's beloved characters jumped from the printed page and onto the silver screen.

Follow the yellow brick road to the corner of Webster Avenue and Larrabee Street, where you'll find the Scarecrow, the Cowardly Lion, the Tin Man, and of course Dorothy and her little dog Toto. Dorothy Melamerson, a Chicago public school physical education teacher, who preferred to live a frugal life, gave the children of her city this cherished 13-plus-acre park as a gift.

The Scarecrow reigns over the park's Emerald Garden. At the southeast corner, the bronze Cowardly Lion proudly displays his badge of courage. Dorothy and Toto watch over the children as they head towards the playground swings and slides. The Tin Man guards the northeast corner, proudly displaying his brand new ticking heart. A wooden Oz play structure features plenty of corners to hide from the wicked witch, as well as slides and swings for big and little munchkins. The statues were all created by John Kearney, a Chicago- and Provincetown-based artist famous for his figurative sculptures made of found metal objects. See if you can spot the old chrome car bumpers that Kearney welded together to bring Oz Park's Tin Man to life.

TIP: Oz Park is one of many Chicago parks that show free outdoor movies as part of the Movies in the Park summer series (www.chicagoparkdistrict.com/movies).

Address 2021 N. Burling Street, Chicago, IL 60614, www.chicagoparkdistrict.com/parks // Getting there Brown or Purple Line to Armitage // Hours Daily 6am–11pm // Ages 3+

79_ PARTICLE ACCEL-ERATOR AND A BISON HERD

Big physics on the prairie at Fermilab

Fermi National Accelerator Laboratory, or Fermilab, in west suburban Batavia, is a United States Department of Energy national laboratory best known for high-energy particle physics research. As you hike or bike the 1,000 acres of restored tallgrass prairie that surrounds the tallest building on site, the uniquely shaped Wilson Hall, it's hard to believe that you're likely standing upon what was once the most powerful particle accelerator in the world, used by scientists to discover what makes up our unfolding universe.

Hike or bike the quarter-mile-long Margaret Pearson Interpretive Trail which connects to several miles of trails through woodland, restored oak savanna, and tallgrass prairie. You'll likely encounter animal life along the way: the lab's grounds are home to eastern tiger salamanders, Baltimore orioles, and great spangled fritillary, which are large orange butterflies with black markings.

Pause at the Bison Pasture and Viewing area, which overlooks an 80-acre pasture populated by the lab's very own herd of buffalo. Fermi's first director, Robert R. Wilson, introduced the bison in 1969. Today, the herd of about 25 bison roams the prairie here, giving a glimpse of what the area looked like hundreds of years ago.

Take a tour of Wilson Hall, where, from the 15th floor, you can step inside the control room packed with computers and also see the four-mile ring of water that marks the particle accelerator's location and the Chicago skyline miles away in the distance.

TIP: Nearby Garfield Farm and Inn Museum is an 1840s prairie farmstead and inn that now operates as a working farm museum.

Address Pine Street and Kirk Road, Batavia, IL 60510, +1 (630) 840-8258, www.fnal.gov/pub/visiting, fermilab@fnal.gov // Getting there From Chicago, travel west on the Eisenhower (I-290) to I-88. Exit I-88 at the Farnsworth exit, north or right. Farnsworth becomes Kirk Road. Follow Kirk Road to Pine Street. Turn right at Pine Street, Fermilab's main entrance. // Hours See website // Ages 3+

80 _ PERRY MASTODON

Mighty mastodon

Once upon a time, mighty mastodons, ancient ancestors of today's elephants, roamed North America. Around 11,000 years ago, a mature, healthy female mastodon was wandering what is today Glen Ellyn, Illinois, when she attempted to cross an icy lake. As the ice below her shattered, she fractured her right leg bones and fell to her death, settling at the bottom of the lake for what would have been an eternity.

It wasn't until 1963 that a construction worker digging an artificial pond discovered a mega-sized bone in the bucket of his excavator. Wheaton College faculty and students later recovered 118 bone fragments and 92 full bones of the long-dead lady mastodon. Since the property was owned by US District Court Judge Joseph Sam Perry, the reconstructed skeleton was named Perry Mastodon. Later, scientists discovered that Perry was actually a female, but her name stuck.

Today, Perry Mastodon lives on at the new Meyer Science Center's interactive atrium museum. Standing tall, her missing bones were replaced by fiberglass, so kids can experience the mightiness of this oversized, ancient, forest-dwelling animal. One half of Perry is reconstructed with skin on her bones, so it's easy to imagine exactly what she looked like long ago, when Illinois was in the midst of the Ice Age.

Mastodons lived in herds and grazed, similar to elephants. Though Perry died in an unfortunate accident, her fellow mastodons eventually disappeared from North America as part of a mass extinction, likely caused by over-hunting by humans.

Address 450-598 Howard Street, Wheaton, IL 60187, +1 (630) 752-5000, www.wheaton.edu/about-wheaton/visit-wheaton/campus-buildings/meyer-science-center // Getting there Metra UP-W to College Avenue // Hours Mon–Sat 7am–11pm // Ages 3+

TIP: Nearby, the Clocktower Mini Golf & Skate Park has an 18-hole, prairie-themed mini golf course, and a 12,000-square-foot skate park with areas for beginners and advanced skaters.

81_ PING TOM BOATHOUSE

Boatloads of fun

Chicago's Chinatown is a vibrant ethnic enclave that will transport you direct to Hong Kong via the South Side.

Head to Ping Tom Park to experience the beating (green) heart of Chicago's Chinatown. Its new boathouse incorporates elements of Chinese architecture, from the deep red-colored storage shed with its decorative screens, to the river's edge, with its iconic red Chinese ornamental railings that extend over the water lined with limestone rocks called scholar's stones from Lake Tai in China. The park's entrance is marked by four tall columns, each etched with Chinese dragons. A children's playground is located at the north end of the park. "I'm incredibly proud to raise my family in the Chinatown neighborhood of Chicago," shares M. J. Tam, local mom and editor at Chicagonista.com.

Rent a single or double kayak or set off on a guided journey. The boathouse is run by outdoor outfitter REI, and staff members are happy to offer basic instruction and advice for paddles that fit your family's endurance levels. There was a time not too long ago when the Chicago River was so polluted that a kayak excursion was next to impossible. But with the help of organizations like Friends of the Chicago River, Chicago's central waterway is slowly working its way back to health. Paddle towards downtown and see if you can spot a heron stalking the shallows for fish, a turtle basking on a log, or a family of ducks enjoying an excursion of their own.

Address 19th Street and Wells Street, Chicago, IL 60616, +1 (312) 339 7669, www.rei.com/h/ping-tom-boathouse, chicagoboathouse@rei.com // Getting there Red Line to Cermak-Chinatown // Hours See website for seasonal hours // Ages 3+

TIP: The best time of year to visit is in the summertime, when the boathouse plays host to the Chicago Dragon Boat Race for Literacy, an event that pits dragon-shaped boats against one another to promote local literacy, cultural, and diversity programs.

82_POO FOUNTAIN

Remember to scoop your poop

Poo. Everybody does it. Everybody deals with it. One artist in Chicago decided to sculpt an ode to poop in all its brown, semi-solid, stinky glory.

This crappy yet oddly inspiring water fountain was a gift to the Ukrainian Village community from Polish-American sculptor Jerzy S. Kenar, who topped a tiled base with a beautiful swirl of doggie doo-doo from which a gentle stream of water flows. *Shit Fountain* is poetically inscribed on its base.

Created and installed just off the sidewalk in a tiny courtyard in 2005, Kenar's main aim was to remind walkers to pick up their dog's dastardly dung. It's one thing to admire a bronze BM, but we can all agree that no one wants to step in it. Plus, rats love to eat fresh, steamy dog poops. This delightful fountain is a vivid call out to dog-toting passersby to pack a pooper scooper so that our streets remain clean and vermin-free.

Kenar told *Time Out Chicago* that his poop installation was "dedicated to all the dogs in Chicago," dogs who, if they could, would certainly pick up after themselves.

Kenar, an immigrant from Poland via Sweden, hasn't always focused on fecal matter. Owner of the Wooden Gallery, he's also done work for a number of churches in the Chicago area and even created the stunning Millennium Doors for 'Chicago's Polish Cathedral,' Holy Trinity Church.

TIP: Kenar also created the nearby Barn Angel, a heavenly angel carved of wood, now imprisoned by protective iron bars, at the corner of Wolcott Avenue and Augusta Boulevard.

Address 1001 N. Wolcott
Avenue, Chicago, IL 60622 //
Getting there Blue Line to
Division // Hours Unrestricted //
Ages 3+

SHIT FO

83_ PRETTY COOL

Cool as ice

You're pretty cool and you know it. Celebrate your cool attitude with a rainbow of icy treats at Pretty Cool, a whimsical, colorful, playful, and just plain cool ice cream shop that doesn't sell by the scoop.

Instead, the 50+ ice cream novelties are a gourmet take on what you'd find on an old-school Good Humor truck, served skewered with a wooden Popsicle-style stick.

The bars and ice pops here are classified into five cool categories. Custard Bars are ice cream submerged in chocolate, with flavors ranging from the classic – vanilla, cookies and cream – to the exotic – peanut butter potato chip, coffee pretzel toffee. Truck Pops transform the standard ice pop with inventive flavors, such as litchi lemon tea and passion fruit hibiscus. Plant Pops are vegan-friendly, creamy treats made with non-dairy milks. Magic Shell-inspired Party Pops are cream cheese bars dipped into Pretty Cool's proprietary shell blend and topped with sprinkles.

Pony Pops are made with tiny appetites and little hands in mind. Smaller in size, they're available in classic, kid-friendly flavors – vanilla custard, strawberry buttermilk, chocolate custard, grape pop, and pink lemonade pop – and cost $2 each.

Chef and founder Dana Salls Cree also kept kids in mind when it came to the design of the store. "A lot of the touches in the shop have been to make it inviting to children without turning it into a playground," she told the *Chicago Tribune* just before the shop opened in August, 2018. "The sight line of the cases are low enough for little eyes," she added. "We built this stadium-style seating, we envision kids climbing up and down. We put a window into the production area with a ledge that kids can climb up on and watch."

Address 2353 N. California Avenue, Chicago, IL 60647, +1 (773) 697-4140, www.prettycoolicecream.com, info@prettycoolicecream.com // Getting there Blue Line to California // Hours Daily, see website for seasonal hours // Ages 3+

TIP: Don't forget to bring Fido along for the ride. Pupsicles are taste tested by Salls Cree's corgi.

84_ QING XIANG YUAN DUMPLINGS

Jiǎozi galore

Everybody loves dumplings. Whether you call them ravioli, pierogi, momo, or gyoza, dumplings are one of those foods that pop up in the kitchens of just about every culture around the world. At Qing Xiang Yuan Dumplings, QXY for short, jiǎozi with dozens of different fillings are handmade daily.

QXY started out as a small stand in a basement food court but soon developed such a cult following that they moved dumpling operations to this sleek, sunny spot at the southeastern edge of the Chinatown Square shopping mall.

Flip through the iPad menu, where pictures make it easy for even pre-readers to make their selections in style, to discover the dumplings of the day. The chicken-and-coriander and beef-and-onion dumplings are guaranteed kid-pleasers, but give some of the more interesting fillings a try: scallops and lotus root, sea cucumber, sea urchin, lobster, and crab roe. Then let your server know if you prefer your dumplings steamed or pan-fried.

Every dumpling here is formed and folded to order, and you can watch it all unfold thanks to a window that frames the busy kitchen. Even better, take your skills a step further and sign up to make your own dumpling dinner – QXY hosts several dumpling-making classes every week. Kids will enjoy learning the traditional methods of filling, folding, and sealing dumplings, and you'll be able to eat 12 of your creations or opt to take them home.

TIP: Shelves overflow with woks, sea sponges, ceremonial incense, tea sets, ceramic Chinese zodiac figurines, lanterns, Pokémon cards, stuffed animals, lucky bamboo shoots, and more at AJ Housewares & Gifts, also located in the Chinatown Square Mall.

Address 2002 S. Wentworth
Avenue 103, Chicago,
IL 60616, +1 (312) 799-1118,
www.qxydumplings.com,
contact@qxydumplings.com //
Getting there Red Line to
Cermak-Chinatown // Hours
Daily 11:30am–9pm // Ages 3+

85_RAINBOW BEACH DUNES

A glimpse of the South Shore, circa 1800

When people think of dunes, they often think of Indiana's towering sand hills. But at the southernmost corner of Rainbow Beach, a 10.2-acre dune habitat thrives with native grasses, wildflowers, and singing birds. Try your best to ignore the picture-perfect views of Chicago's skyline for a moment, as this incredible ecosystem offers a glimpse of what the shoreline looked like long ago, before the city expanded and became the bustling metropolis that it is today.

This formerly grassy stretch has been slowly reclaimed by native species, and a natural dune began forming as sand blown in by the wind formed a stable ridge. Some ecologists believe that the seeds for native dune grasses may have traveled from Indiana Dunes National Lakeshore. The Chicago Park District stepped in to help the process along, renaming the area Rainbow Beach Dunes and declaring it a bird and butterfly sanctuary and natural dune.

A 0.8-mile trail – the perfect length hike for little legs – loops around the dune and the adjacent wetlands that are slowly returning to life in response to the restoration efforts by volunteers who have been cutting brush, removing invasive species, and planting native seeds. As you walk on the dune pathway, note the amazing diversity of plant life. One of the rarest plants that now lives here is the prickly pear cactus, also known as Opuntia Humifusa.

Rainbow Beach was the site of several Civil Rights 'wade ins', when young and diverse activists stepped onto its shores, declaring the right for everyone to enjoy a day at the beach.

Address 3111 E. 77th Street, Chicago, IL 60649, +1 (630) 213-2277, www.chicagoparkdistrict.com/parks-facilities/rainbow-beach-park // Getting there CTA bus 26 to S. Shore Drive & 77th Street // Hours Daily 6am–11pm // Ages 3+

TIP: Nearby is Park 566, part of the historic US Steel South Works plant and now an amazing place for to spot a wide variety of birds (use Rainbow Beach entrance).

86_THE RINK
Marvelous moves on wheels

Roller skating offers a meditative moment on wheels: tie on your roller skates, step onto the smooth maple floor, and lose yourself to the music and your best moves.

Chicago, together with Atlanta and Detroit, birthed the urban roller-skate dance scene in the country. While this form of skating is largely influenced by hip-hop music and dance, Chicago's style of skating is known as 'JB' for its pairing of city-born hip-hop and James Brown-inspired beats with fancy, intricate footwork. The best place in the city to see these marvelous moves in action is at The Rink. Opened in 1975, it's perhaps the most storied rink in the city. It even served as a backdrop in the 1997 comedy-drama hit movie *Soul Food*, writer and director George Tillman, Jr.'s major studio debut.

"It just signifies what Black culture is: family, love, pride, passion, and enjoyment," long-time skater Patrice Jackson told Chicago Public Radio in a 2019 profile of the popular venue.

Two skating rinks – a main skating rink and a practice rink – bustle with passionate skaters showcasing the hottest moves in town. If you or your kids are new to roller skating, The Rink offers lessons for learners of all ages, keeping the tradition alive for future generations of roller skaters. It's also a popular birthday party destination for bigs and littles.

When you need to take a breather, you can play pool on one of the two regulation pool tables, or head up to the smaller third floor which is reserved for dancing your heart out – without your wheels.

> TIP: If you prefer zooming around on in-liners, the best place to blade in the city is along the Chicago Lakefront Trail, the 18.5-mile path that runs from near the 63rd Street Beach to the northernmost edge of Lincoln Park.

Address 1122 E. 87th Street, Chicago, IL 60619, +1 (773) 221-2600, www.therinkchicago.com, contacttherink@therinkchicago.com // Getting there Metra ME to 87th Street/Woodruff // Hours Daily 9am–midnight, see website for open skate times // Ages 3+

87 _ROBIE HOUSE

The Wright Three had the right stuff

In Blue Balliet's award-winning children's novel *The Wright Three,* sixth-graders Calder and Petra live in Chicago's Hyde Park and attend the real-life University of Chicago Laboratory Schools when their teacher announces that Frank Lloyd Wright's 1910 Robie House, a 20th-century American architectural masterpiece, is about to be demolished. Shocked that a neighborhood icon is about to vanish for good, the tweens set off to save Robie House, only to be drawn into a developing mystery involving secret messages, potential ghosts, and a puzzle that can only be solved with true teamwork and a little help from Calder's pentominoes and Fibonacci numbers.

Alongside the mystery and fun in the novel, young readers are asked to ponder the importance of historic preservation.

Frank Lloyd Wright designed Robie House, considered a classic example of Wright's Prairie School-style architecture, for forward-thinking Frederick Robie, a bicycle and motorcycle manufacturer. The plans unfolded in Wright's Oak Park studio in 1908. The home, completed in 1910, is considered a forerunner of modernism in architecture and is one of Wright's most celebrated designs.

Preface a visit to Robie House with a reading of the novel, and then set off on a 40-minute guided tour to see the hallowed halls and rooms where Calder and Petra's ghostly plot unfolded and learn all the real secrets of Wright's timeless and revolutionary Prairie-style masterpiece.

> **TIP:** *The Sixty-Eight Rooms,* a four-book series written by Marianne Malone that follows the adventures of two sixth-graders in Chicago who discover a magic key that allows them to shrink to fit inside Thorne Miniature Rooms (see ch. 101).

Address 5757 S. Woodlawn
Avenue, Chicago, IL 60637,
+1 (312) 994-4000,
www.flwright.org/visit/
robiehouse, info@flwright.org //
Getting there Tours offered
Thu–Mon 10am–3pm, reserve
online // **Hours** Metra ME
to University of Chicago/59th
Street // **Ages 8+**

88__ROGERS PARK ORB
Mysterious selfie sphere

Once upon a time, in 2018, a mysterious orb landed on Juneway Beach Park in Rogers Park. Perfectly smooth and shiny, the 700-pound sphere seemed to have arrived from another planet altogether.

Was it an alien spaceship? A little sister to Millennium Park's bean? A strange moon that dropped from outer space? A portal to another universe?

Ask your kids where they think the orb came from, and you'll surely hear some great guesses. Kids love peering into its reflective, polished steel surface, where they can catch a funny, round image of themselves with the wide expanse of Lake Michigan as a backdrop. The small stretch of sandy beach and the surrounding park make this a great spot for a quiet, beachside picnic too.

The surprise orb is actually *Quantum Dee,* a work of art by Davis McCarty and part of the 50 x 50 Neighborhood Arts Project, in which the City of New York commissioned local artists to create site-specific works of public art for each of Chicago's 50 wards. McCarty created the orb and the dichroic plexiglass and stainless steel spire that was recently added to support it.

"The sculpture's vibrant colors are representative of the vibrant diverse community in Rogers Park," writes McCarty on Instagram. "This 20-foot gem serves as a gateway landmark on Chicago's lakefront."

Bring your camera: this orb makes fun house-style selfies.

> TIP: Lifeline Theatre offers a rich menu of theatrical and educational programming geared towards children. Many of the featured plays are based on famous children's books.

Address 7519 N. Eastlake Terrace, Chicago,
IL 60626, www.rpba.org/2019/01/quantum-dee //
Getting there Purple, Red, Yellow Line to
Howard // Hours Daily 6am–11pm // Ages 3+

89_ROSENBERG FOUNTAIN

Newsie dream come true

From the mid-19th to the early 20th century, newspapers were distributed by 'newsies,' little boys who purchased the papers from the publishers and sold them as independent agents. Shouting "Extra! Extra!" into the wee hours, the newsboys, many of whom were homeless, tried to sell every last paper they could, as they weren't allowed to return unsold copies. They typically earned only about 30 cents a day.

In 1866, a reformer named Charles Loring Brace wrote of the newsies: "I remember one cold night seeing some 10 or a dozen of the little homeless creatures piled together to keep each other warm beneath the stairway of The [New York] Sun office. There used to be a mass of them also at The Atlas office, sleeping in the lobbies, until the printers drove them away by pouring water on them."

Joseph Rosenberg (1848–1891) worked as a newsie in Gilded Age Chicago when he was just a little boy. On hot days, when he became very thirsty, he had a hard time finding a merchant that would spare him a sip of water. He vowed that one day, should he grow up to be a rich man, he'd create a fountain where everyone was welcome to a cool drink of water.

Rosenberg did become a wealthy man. Following through with his promise, he left a $10,000 bequest for an ornamental drinking fountain in Grant Park, near his childhood home. Today Hebe, the Goddess of Youth, cupbearer to the gods, continues to offer a cup of water to anyone in need.

Address Grant Park, east of S. Michigan Avenue and just south of E. 11th Street, Chicago, IL 60605, www.chicagoparkdistrict.com/parks-facilities/grant-park // Getting there Red, Green, or Orange Line to Roosevelt // Hours Daily 6am–11pm // Ages 3+

TIP: At the southern end of Grant Park, stands *Agora* by artist Magdalena Abakanowicz, 106 10-foot-tall torsos that appear to walk and stand in groups. Kids will love getting lost among the maze of iron sculptures.

90 _ SAGAWAU CANYON

Just-as-grand canyon

The Grand Canyon is certainly grand. But did you know there's a magnificent canyon to explore in Chicagoland's backyard? Trek on over to Lemont, where the lush Sagawau Canyon, the only such landform in northeastern Illinois, will transport you to the days of the dinosaurs.

It's hard to believe that once upon a time, this gorge was a bustling coral reef. Located in the valley of the Des Plaines River, the exposed dolomite rock that the gorge is carved through is likely the reason why biodiversity rules this smaller-scale canyon. Indeed, the bulblet fern, purple cliff brake (another fern family member), walking fern, hairy rock cress, and ninebark thrive in this rock-rich environment and create a backdrop that appears more Jurassic Park and less suburban Chicago. The stream that runs through the canyon tumbles over a waterfall and winds through the forest in a cobbled stream bed. The canyon's 20-foot-high sandstone walls create the just-right conditions to support the rare plants and animals that live here and only here. Keep your eyes on the lookout for the many canyon residents, which include blue-spotted salamanders, eastern tiger salamanders, mudpuppies, map turtles, soft-shell turtles, milk snakes, green snakes, flying squirrels, minks, long-tailed weasels, beavers, and gray and red foxes. The best way to explore the canyon is on a naturalist-guided hike, offered weekly throughout the year.

There are a few clues to this area's prehistoric past: fossils galore can be found among the canyon's ancient stones, especially at the edge of the stream, including the imprint of a cephaloid (the ancestor of today's squid). It's forbidden to take any fossils home with you.

TIP: Take a moment to explore Lemont's historic Main Street, where you'll find quaint shops and cafes housed in 19th-century buildings.

Address 12545 111th Street, Lemont, IL 60439, +1 (630) 257-2045, www.fpdcc.com/venue/sagawau-environmental-learning-center // **Getting there** Follow I-90 E/I-94 E and I-55 S to IL-83 S/Kingery Highway in Downers Grove Township. Take exit 274 from I-55 S. Follow IL-83 S about four miles to the canyon entrance. // **Hours** Daily 8am–4pm // **Ages** 3+

91_ SAN SOO GAB SAN

Royal feast by fire

For the family that likes to feast like kings and queens, Korean barbecue palace San Soo Gab San is fit for royalty. Don't let its strip mall location or simple decor fool you – this restaurant is not only one of the best dining spots in town, it's also the most authentic. The kitchen, thankfully, won't bow down to Western sensibilities, so you know you're tasting tradition.

The only non-royal part about this feast? You'll have to cook your own feast – at your table. But it's worth your efforts - San Soo Gab San was named to Michelin's Bib Gourmand list.

Kids love this, of course. Under the careful supervision of Mom and Dad, they can slowly roast their choice of meats on the tabletop, charcoal grill. Shared plates and tabletop cooking mean you can cuddle close or get your wiggles out whenever.

The menu is extensive, but the marinated, grill-your-own meats are the stars. Bulgogi, beef tenderloin marinated in soy sauce, sugar, sesame oil, garlic and pepper, and *galbi*, beef short ribs marinated in soy sauce, water, garlic, sugar and sliced onions, are the most popular.

Before your meat arrives, your server will gift you with twenty-plus *banchan* (side dishes) - some are sweet, some are savory, and all of them are delicious. Each is served in a small white bowl, making for a fun tasting adventure. Who knows? Your kids might find a new healthy favorite from the many blanched, steamed, braised, or stir-fried vegetable sides.

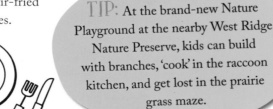

TIP: At the brand-new Nature Playground at the nearby West Ridge Nature Preserve, kids can build with branches, 'cook' in the raccoon kitchen, and get lost in the prairie grass maze.

Address 5247 N. Western Avenue, Chicago, IL 60625, +1 (773) 334-1589, www.ssgsbbq.com // Getting there Brown Line to Western, then CTA bus 49 or X49 to Western & Foster // Hours Fri & Sat 11–2am, Sun–Thu, 11–1am // Ages 3+

92_ SOLAR-POWERED PYRAMID

The future is bright in Bronzeville

Pyramids rose in ancient Egypt as tombs for pharaohs and queens.

Here in Chicago, a new pyramid gathers energy from the sun to generate enough power to glow at night. This collaboration between ComEd, the largest electric utility in Illinois, a local artist, an art gallery, and a team of brilliant high-school students puts the spotlight on Bronzeville, where it lights up 446 E. 47th Street, reminding everyone that the future is bright if we work together and share our gifts.

Each of the pyramid's black solar-powered panels features design elements that represented the individual personalities of the children that took part in the project. Look for a panda bear, a butterfly, an owl wearing a crown, a lightbulb, the eye of Horus, and many others on each side of the pyramid.

The solar-powered artwork was created by local artist Olusola Akintunde, or Shala, who guided the children in a lesson in STEM via the arts through ComEd's Solar Spotlight Education Program. Gallery Guichard joined in on the construction of the pyramid, which now collects sun in the garden next door.

"I think the pyramid will inspire people," Shala said. "People have always felt that a lot of power comes from pyramids, especially in ancient times. A pyramid also has a strong foundation. That imagery will mean something to people."

Address 450 E. 47th Street, Chicago, IL 60653 // Getting there Green Line to 47th Street // Hours Unrestricted // Ages 3+

TIP: Don't leave E. 47th Street before popping into Abundance Bakery for a dozen of their signature dessert, Uncle Villy's Upside-Down Caramel Cupcakes.

93_ STEELWORKERS' MERMAID

Siren of the lake

In 1985, a mermaid washed up upon the shores of Lake Michigan.

She stretches peacefully atop her limestone boulder perch, her eyes closed to avoid the sun's rays, curved long hair swaying into the stone-carved waves. She seems to be resting after a particularly treacherous swim to shore.

No one knew where she came from, but there were plenty of guesses. Maybe she was a long lost piece of sculpture from the 1893 Columbian Exhibition? Maybe she once graced a Gilded Era mansion?

The truth is she was made by four out-of-work steelworkers.

Roman Villarreal was one of 16,000 area steelworkers who lost their jobs between 1979 and 1986.

"That period led to the downfall of many, many good men in South Chicago who were steelworkers," Villarreal told the *South Side Weekly* in 2015. "I was fortunate enough that I had odd goals in my mind. Art was my savior because I was able to concentrate a lot of my energy into my art projects."

Roman sketched a mermaid using his daughter as a model and then convinced his steelworker buddies Jose Moreno, Fred Arroyo, and Edfu Kingigna to bring her to life in sculpture. The mermaid marked a move into the world of art for Villareal, who paints and sculpts and teaches art to this day.

In 2010, she swam ashore here to Oakwood Beach, where you can find her resting upon the shores of Lake Michigan, a mysterious mermaid much loved by locals.

TIP: Walk about a mile south on Lakefront Trail to the Burnham Nature Center and explore a test plot of prairie wildflowers and the Butterfly Garden.

Address Near the bike path at Oakwood-41st Street Beach, 4100 S. Lake Shore Drive, Chicago, IL 60653 // Getting there Metra ME to 47th Street (Kenwood) // Hours Daily dawn–dusk // Ages 3+

94_SUPERDAWG DRIVE-IN

Red hot love

It's easy to spot Superdawg in the distance as you drive along Milwaukee Avenue with two 12-foot-tall hot dogs – Maurie, a muscular, caveman-style red hot, and his sweetheart Flaurie, her sausage crown topped with a big blue bow – dancing on the rooftop. These two weenies have been overseeing the cars that pull in and out of this classic carport-style drive-in since the 1950s, when Superdawg was a cruisin' hotspot.

Though there are hundreds of places in the city where you can find an authentic Chicago-style hot dogs, nothing beats driving into Superdawg on a summer night. Pull into the one of the carports, roll down your window, place your order into the retro speakerbox, and wait for your waitress to clip your tray to your window. Then proceed to enjoy the delectable dogs, hand-cut fries and rich Supermalts, all from the comfort of your car.

Superdawg first opened in May, 1948, not long after Maurie Berman, a recently returned G.I. from World War II, married his high-school sweetheart Florence (Flaurie). Since Maurie was attending Northwestern University and Flaurie was teaching at a Chicago public school, the newlyweds decided to open a roadside hot dog stand, hoping to make some extra money during the summer months. Inspired by popular superheroes of the 1940s, they named their new business Superdawg.

Today, Berman's kids and grandkids run the show at this beloved restaurant, where countless families have created fond memories.

Address 6363 N. Milwaukee Avenue, Chicago, IL 60646, +1 (773) 763-0660, www.superdawg.com, contactus@superdawg.com // Getting there Blue Line to Jefferson Park, then CTA bus 270 to Nagle & Milwaukee // Hours Sun–Thu 11–1am, Fri & Sat 11–2am // Ages 3+

95_ SURF LAKE MICHIGAN

Check out those rad barrels at Montrose Beach

Did you know you can hang ten in Chicago?!

For many, "Life's a beach." For others, "Life's a wave." Thankfully, there's no need to catch the next flight to Oahu. Lake Michigan's waves are wind powered, and the Windy City makes for waves year-round.

Unlike their ocean cousins, our waves are salt-free, come in quicker succession, and are less powerful, making for ideal 'first surf' conditions. All you need is a kid-sized surfboard, a life vest, and breezy but not too gusty winds. You might also want to don a wetsuit, as Lake Michigan's water temps average about 75.5°F in the summer.

"It's hard to describe the feeling of surfing, especially the feeling of surfing on an enormous freshwater lake," explains Ryan Gerard, owner of the one and only area surf outfitter, Third Coast Surf. "Paddling out into nature with the fish and the birds, with the Chicago skyline behind you, and riding a wave of energy toward shore brings a joy unlike any that can be found on land."

Surfing is allowed year-round at Montrose and 57th Street beaches, but Gerard recommends Montrose Beach as the most kid-friendly surfing beach in the city. "With its wide expanse of clean white sand, generally smaller waves, and nearby amenities – Montrose is an ideal place for 'groms' (surfing parlance for kid) and their families to catch the surfing bug."

TIP: Third Coast Surf Shop sells and rents boards and wetsuits for kids and adults. They also offer private and group lessons as well as surf-centric summer camps.

Address 4400 N. Lake Shore Drive, Chicago, IL 60613, www.chicagoparkdistrict.com/parks-facilities/montrose-beach // Getting there Red Line to Wilson, then CTA bus 78 to Wilson & Marine Drive // Hours Daily 6am–11pm // Ages 7+

96_ SURPRISE BOOKSHELF

Calling all bookworms

Bookworms big and small will want to make a beeline to Chicago's brand new and amazing American Writers Museum, where a surprise bookshelf brings the words of diverse American writers to life through touch, sound, and even smell.

Located in the museum's Nation of Writers Gallery, this one-of-a-kind, 85-foot-long bookshelf celebrates the diversity of writing forms of America's most iconic authors, from novels to song lyrics to comics and many more. Open up one of the 100 illuminated book placards and expect to be surprised. Flip Stephen Foster's cube to hear *Oh! Susanna.* Turn Harper Lee's to hear the sounds of a mockingbird. Open Julia Child's to smell cookies fresh from the oven. *Fahrenheit 451* by Ray Bradbury flips to reveal books... on fire.

"Kids love the Surprise Bookshelf because of the element of surprise and fun," shared Sonal Shukla, Assistant Director of Programming and Education. "The kids usually go through the entire exhibit looking for the 'surprises' that have the element of smell in them."

Beyond the Surprise Bookshelf, check out the dedicated children's literature room, where comfy couches invite little ones to curl up with a good book. See if your kids can spot some of the children's classics depicted by Caldecott Medal-winning author and illustrator Paul O. Zelinsky in his large-scale mural that depicts book-loving squirrels in a grand tree. Six small-scale exhibits highlight famous American children's books, including *Little House on the Prairie, Where the Wild Things Are,* and *Charlotte's Web.*

Address 180 N. Michigan Avenue, Chicago, IL 60601, +1 (312) 374-8790, www.americanwritersmuseum.org // Getting there Brown, Orange, Pink, Purple, or Green Line to State/Lake // Hours Daily 10am–5pm // Ages 3+

TIP: Extend your reading adventures with a visit to the Harold Washington Library's Children's Library, a colorful, circus-inspired space complete with a circus train car reading nook and books galore.

97 _ SUSHI + ROTARY SUSHI BAR

Sushi on wheels

Imagine a restaurant where all of your favorite foodie dishes are spinning around you almost non-stop, tempting you with their deliciousness. And best of all, you can take what you'd like and wait for another favorite to spin by you in just a few minutes. At Sushi + Rotary Sushi Bar, the dishes – mostly beautifully presented sushi bites, but also drinks, soups, desserts, and other delights – are placed onto a slim conveyor belt that snakes around the dining area. A steady stream of over 90 different dishes travel along the belt from the kitchen before they end up in the bellies of eager diners.

Sushi is the star of the show here, and it's never too early to introduce the kid in your life to Dragon Ballz, spicy crab *gunkan*, and sweet potato *maki*. Other kid-approved dishes that make the rounds include *gyoza* (fried, meat-filled dumplings), crunchy *edamame*, warm miso soup, mango and cheese eggrolls, and Philadelphia maki, a good beginner sushi bite made of smoked salmon, avocado, and cream cheese. Order drinks from the tablet on your table and then simply grab the foods that entice before they pass by you. Color-coded dishes indicate price.

Besides the conveyor belt items, the menu here features ramen soup, stir-fried noodles, and Chinese dishes, like sesame chicken. Bento boxes are also popular here, including kid-sized boxes filled with sushi, teriyaki chicken or beef, as well as rice, French fries, and freshly cut fruit. A speedy, red race car hops on the track to deliver kid bento boxes direct to your table.

Address 3219 N. Broadway Street, Chicago, IL 60657, +1 (872) 802-0980, www.rotarysushi.com // Getting there Brown or Red Line to Belmont // Hours See website for hours // Ages 3+

TIP: Take your science kid to learn about Nicola Tesla in an exhibit dedicated to the life and work of the inventor at the Serbian American Museum St. Sava.

98_SWAN PADDLE BOATS

Set sail for adventure at Humboldt Park Lagoon

Board a giant white swan and head out on a fairy-tale adventure!

You'll step onto your magical vessel at the Prairie-style boathouse and launch into the always serene lagoon. Curious ducks are bound to play in your wake as you paddle along. If you're lucky, you just might spot a real-life swan, or perhaps its longer-necked cousin, the great blue heron, hiding amidst the native plant and flower-lined shores.

Humboldt Park was originally designed in 1871 by William Le Baron Jenney as part of the city's grand, linked boulevard system. Near the boathouse stands a 10-foot-tall monument of the park's namesake, naturalist Alexander von Humboldt. Acclaimed landscape architect Jens Jensen served as superintendent of the park in the late 1890s, finding inspiration for his ground-breaking designs. The Humboldt Park Natural Area is 28.6 acres of gardens, woodland, wetland, prairie, savanna habitats, and a lagoon that call this green corner of Chicago home.

Wheel Fun Rentals offers swan boat rentals at the park in partnership with the Chicago Park District.

A bevy of seven small swan boats each fit two adults or one adult and one kid. Prep for a workout and remember to wear sunscreen and a hat. Kayaks, stand-up paddle boards, and a few different types of bikes are also available for rent. On the other side of the lagoon is the newly redesigned swimming area, Chicago's only inland beach. Save time to cool off with a dip!

Address 1301 N. Humboldt Drive, Chicago, IL 60622 // Getting there Blue Line to California // Hours Daily 6am–11pm // Ages 3+

TIP: Fuel up pre-paddle with *avena de coco* (coconut oatmeal) at Nellie's Puerto Rican Restaurant, a family-owned eatery nestled in the heart of Humboldt Park's vibrant Puerto Rican community.

99__TAHOORA SWEETS AND BAKERY

Taste the sugary, South Asian rainbow

It's no surprise that the Indian subcontinent has developed an almost endless and amazing array of sweets: sugarcane has been grown on the subcontinent for thousands of years, and the art of refining sugar was invented there 8,000 years ago. The English word 'sugar' comes from the ancient Sanskrit word sharkara and the word 'candy' comes from the Sanskrit word khaanda.

At Tahoora, located in Chicago's vibrant Desi Corridor along Devon Avenue, you'll find a rainbow of colorful and traditional subcontinental treats. It's the perfect spot for an afternoon pick-me-up that promises some of the most unique treats this side of Bangalore. Favorites include *besan ladoo*, sweet balls made from chickpea flour, sugar, ghee, and nuts; *burfi*, a type of fudge available in mango, carrot, and the rare *chikoo* fruit. *Mewa* are foil-wrapped, square-shaped bites made from cashews, almonds, and pistachios.

Ball-shaped sweets are very popular here, especially during holidays such as Eid, when it's common to bring a box of sweets to social gatherings. *Falsa* are pink and white milk-based balls with a spongy texture and airy center. 'Cream cutlets' are deep-fried dough balls smothered in cardamom syrup. *Ras gullah* are delightful paneer cheesecake spheres. Some sweets contain no sugar – just ask!

The savory street snacks served here are equally delicious. Kids will love the *pakora* – deep fried veggies – and the *samosas*, deep-fried dumplings stuffed with potatoes and peas. Wash it all down with a lassi, a yogurt drink sweetened with pureed mango.

TIP: Gather armfuls and armfuls of brilliant bangles, most costing less than $1 each, at Salma Fabrics & Boutique.

Address 2345 W. Devon Avenue, Chicago, IL 60659, +1 (773) 743-7272, www.tahoora.com, tahoora@ymail.com // Getting there Brown Line to Western, then CTA bus 49B to Western & Devon // Hours Daily 10am–10pm // Ages 3+

CHAMCHAM

100_ THE TEACHING GREENHOUSE

Green adventures at Kilbourn Park

With American kids spending less than ten minutes a day in unstructured, outdoor play, and an average of seven hours staring at screens, getting out into the great outdoors is more important than ever.

Playing outside helps reduce stress levels, increases critical thinking and problem-solving skills, and helps kids build active, healthy bodies. It's also fun!

Kids are invited to explore the wonderful world of nature at Kilbourn Park, the Chicago Park District's only park with a teaching greenhouse, public orchard, and natural playground.

The park plays host to a tri-season Harvest Garden youth program, a Garden Buddies program for toddlers, and various family gardening workshops throughout the year, but families can pop in anytime to dig around in the verdant greenhouse and gardens. If you're lucky, you might find some apples, pears, plums, cherries, and pawpaws ripe for the picking from the public orchard of trees.

The playground is constructed from all-natural materials – logs, stones, sand, water, wooden tree houses, and wood chip trails – and most elements are movable and can be manipulated for endless creative play. Use the sun to tell the time, thanks to the human sundial. And dig for buried treasure with the wide assortment of shovels and rakes. Garden staff might rope you in to help pick the latest harvest.

As Kilbourn Park Program Specialist Renee Costanzo says, "When kids have a chance to play in native environments, they begin to question why other places are paved over with concrete."

Address 3501 N. Kilbourn Avenue, Chicago, IL 60641, +1 (773) 685-3351 //
Getting there Blue Line to Addison, then CTA bus 152 to Addison & Kilbourn //
Hours Daily 6am–11pm, see website for greenhouse hours // Ages 3+

TIP: Pick up Cuban sandwiches and empanadas at the nearby Bia's Cafe Marianao and enjoy a picnic in the park.

101_THORNE MINIATURE ROOMS

Marvel in miniature

Are you a mouse looking for a house? A doll searching for new digs? Hidden in the lower level of The Art Institute of Chicago, 68 rooms offer some of the most prized real estate in the city.

Decked out in sumptuous period decor ranging from the 13th century to the 1930s, these apartments are exacting replicas of European, American, and Asian interiors, boasting gilded furniture, rich, fabric-lined walls, and golden chandeliers dripping in crystals. But if you're ready to seal a deal with a realtor and move in, think twice. You'll need to be about five inches tall to fit comfortably in these beautiful rooms. That's because they were all designed on a scale of one inch to one foot.

Constructed between 1932 and 1940, the Thorne Miniature Rooms are a celebration of the minuscule. Chicago-based artist Narcissa Niblack Thorne delighted in elegant, historic interiors. She hired top-notch master craftsmen to bring her diminutive dreams to life. Working from her studio, she oversaw every element with an exacting eye. Notice the teeny pieces of fruit that fill the silver bowl in the New Mexico Dining Room, the dog snoozing by the fireplace in the Tudor Great Room, and the hamster-sized instruments in the South Carolina Ballroom.

Before you go, read author Marianne Malone's children's mystery, The Sixty-Eight Rooms, inspired by these tiny interiors.

Address 111 S. Michigan Avenue, Chicago, IL 60603, +1 (312) 443-3600, www.artic.edu // Getting there Brown, Orange, Purple, Pink, or Blue Line to Adams/Wabash // Hours Fri–Wed 10:30am–5pm, Thu 10:30am–8pm // Ages 3+

TIP: Don't forget to stop at the Ryan Education Center in the museum's Modern Wing, where drop-in art activities connect kids to the masterpieces they've just observed.

102_ TREETOP JOURNEY AT GO APE

Zipline adventure

Make like an ape and take a journey through the treetops with Go Ape, an adventure course based out of Bemis Woods.

The Treetop Journey Course is the perfect introduction to high ropes monkey business. Expect to climb straight up to the canopy where you'll experience tree-to-tree crossings, including more than 18 obstacles and two zip lines, at a maximum height of 20 feet above the ground. With the breeze at your back, the tall treetops above, and the ground far below your feet, this is a course that will thrill even the most daring of kids.

The course takes approximately one hour to complete. There's no minimum age requirement, but kids do have to meet the one meter height requirement. Safety systems keep kids attached for the duration of the journey, so there is no need for kids to move any safety lines at all.

Finally, parents, this is an activity that can't be observed from the ground, so plan on conquering your fear of heights once and for all by hooking up to a harness and making like a mama or papa gorilla on the go. One adult must supervise every two children age 5 and under on the course, or up to eight 6–15-year-olds. 16- and 17-year-olds do not require a participating adult, but they do require a waiver signed by their legal guardian.

> TIP: The 400-acres of woods are home to deer and a large variety of birds. Bring binoculars and hike the paved Salt Creek trail, which snakes more than six miles through scenic woods.

Address South Bemis Woods, 1100 Ogden Avenue, Western Springs, IL 60558, +1 (800) 971-8271, www.goape.com // Getting there Metra BNSF to Western Springs // Hours See website for seasonal hours and reservations // Ages 3+

Real isn't how you are made

"There was once a velveteen rabbit, and in the beginning he was really splendid. He was fat and bunchy, as a rabbit should be; his coat was spotted brown and white, he had real thread whiskers, and his ears were lined with pink sateen." So begins The Velveteen Rabbit, the cherished children's story written by Margery Williams in 1922. It tells the tale of what it means to be our authentic selves and embrace love. In 2005, the City of Chicago and the Chicago Park District jointly received a grant from the Illinois Department of Natural Resources to build a new playground in Palmer Square Park. The project called for play equipment geared towards two- to five-year-old children that would reflect the surrounding natural landscape – shady, tall trees and footpaths – and the historic charm of the Palmer Square neighborhood. The team chose *The Velveteen Rabbit* as inspiration, and artists Roman Villarreal, Phil Schuster, and Jennifer Gutowski worked with local children to design and create the artworks.

This is a park where toddlers and preschoolers can take the stage – literally – thanks to the stage-like platform lined with bas relief designs of toys. A carved stone frog, fox, owl, and rabbit, as well as a leafy tree trunk-shaped bench serve as seating and make for outstanding picnic-style dining. Tots can hone their balance upon stepping stones and climb the turtle-like mound. A no-fall, short slide is made for beginners. The tree trunk of a throne is the perfect spot for a regal mom or dad to catch all the action.

Address 2200 N. Kedzie Avenue, Chicago, IL 60647, +1 (312) 742-7535 // Getting there Blue Line to California // Hours Daily 6am–11pm // Ages 3+

TIP: Grab a cup of Miko's Italian Ice to go. It's sweet, refreshing, and made from a range of in-season fruit. Go for the watermelon or the classic lemon.

104_ VIKING LONGSHIP

What would Leif Ericson do?

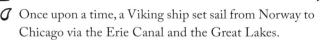

Once upon a time, a Viking ship set sail from Norway to Chicago via the Erie Canal and the Great Lakes.

The 76.5-foot-long, 17-foot-wide ship wasn't built during the Viking Age (793–1066 A.D.), but rather in 1892–1893. An exact replica of the ancient Viking ship discovered in Gokstad, Norway, in 1883, this mighty, seafaring longship was one of the stars of the World's Columbian Exposition in Chicago and is the largest remaining artifact of the grand fair that put Chicago on the map as a center of not just commerce, but also culture.

Though the expo was named after Christopher Columbus, it was likely the Vikings, fierce Scandinavian warriors and explorers, and not an Italian via Spain, who first arrived from Europe to what is today considered North America. Indeed, archaeological evidence of an early Norse settlement in Newfoundland proves that the 'New World' was discovered by the Vikings more than 500 years before Columbus.

Proud Norwegians built an exact duplicate of the storied longship and sailed it 3,000 miles across the Atlantic Ocean, straight to the heart of the exposition in Chicago, Jackson Park.

After the fair, the ship made its way to landlocked Geneva, Illinois, where it remains almost hidden by its protective tent in Good Templar Park, its dragon features not on display.

On select Saturdays, docent-led tours showcase the ship's vibrant history. From a ramp, you can look directly into the hull of the ship, where it's easy to imagine warriors rowing in stride.

TIP: See if you can spot any gnomes hiding among the many tiny, Swedish-inspired, family-owned Cottages in the Woods, located just to the north of the Viking Ship.

Address 528 East Side
Drive, Geneva, IL 60134,
+1 (630) 232-4208,
www.vikingship.us,
viking1893@gmail.com //
Getting there Metra UP-W
to Geneva, IL, then Pace
bus 801 to State Street
& 3rd Street // Hours
See website for hours
and tours // Ages 5+

105_ WATERFALL GLEN FOREST PRESERVE

Hike the trails in an ecological wonderland

Set off on a hike through one of the most ecologically interesting corners of Chicagoland, where four easy-to-hike trails wind through prairies, savannas, and oak-maple woodlands. The 2,503-acre Waterfall Glen Forest Preserve in Darien is best known for its cascading Rocky Glen Waterfall, but few people realize that it's an ecological marvel, home to 740 native plant species and 300 species of mammals, birds, fish, amphibians, and reptiles and counting. Seasonally, over 300 invertebrates make use of this beautiful preserve as a vacation spot of sorts during their migrations.

Three trails that are short on distance but long on splendid sights to see are the Tear-Thumb Trail (1.1 miles), which winds through a vibrant marsh system; the Kettle Hole Trail (0.9 mile), named after the small lake formed long ago from the melting of a mass of ice trapped in glacial deposits; and the Rocky Glen Trail (0.2 mile), which leads to the waterfall.

Ambitious families with older kids will want to take on the 9.5-mile-long Main Trail, which circles the entire preserve, but walk along it for just one mile and you'll meet the magical waterfall.

Hikes here offer prime birdwatching opportunities, so be on the lookout for the wonderful and diverse woodpeckers, scarlet tanagers, ovenbirds, wood thrushes, broad-winged hawks, and barred owls.

Address Northgate Road, Darien, IL 60561, +1 (630) 933-7200, dupageforest.
org/places-to-go/forest-preserves/waterfall-glen, forest@dupageforest.org //
Getting there From I-55, take Cass Avenue 0.5 mile south to Northgate Road.
Turn right on Northgate and go 400 feet to the lot. // Hours Daily
dawn–dusk // Ages 3+

TIP: Several old quarries scattered throughout the preserve offer still fishing waters, so bring your fishing poles! Note that anglers aged 16 or older who are not legally disabled must carry valid Illinois fishing licenses.

106_ WICKER PARK SECRET AGENT SUPPLY CO.

Become Bond, James Bond

If you need to master the art of disguise, catch a crook, or uncover a double agent, you'll find everything you need at Wicker Park Secret Agent Supply Co. It's a small spy shop that conceals a hidden agenda: to amplify the voices of Chicago youth by supporting them with their creative and expository writing skills.

It's easy to be fooled into thinking that this is a spy store for industry insiders thanks to its outstanding inventory of spy gear. Every good spy needs a Sherlock Holmes-style deerstalker cap, rearview glasses, a glue-on handlebar mustache, and a magnifying glass. This secret shop carries all that and more. Up your spy game with a pigeon mask to fool dastardly bird brains, secret service-style earbuds to detect evil plots, or a safe disguised as a Coca-Cola bottle to stash your emergency cash.

Part of a national network of nonprofits started by author Dave Eggers and former teacher Ninive Calegari, Wicker Park Secret Agent Supply Co. is the (store) front for 826CHI, a nonprofit organization that offers free creative writing and homework help services to students ages 6–18. Volunteers here are aptly referred to as 'spies.'

While you can always shop for spy goods that support 826CHI's programming, kids will want to give one of the many creative workshops a try or pop in for some afterschool tutoring fun. The store also carries chapbooks that showcase student writing.

Address 1276 N. Milwaukee Avenue, Chicago, IL 60622, +1 (773) 772-8108, www.secretagentsupply.com, info@826chi.org // Getting there Blue Line to Division // Hours Mon–Sat 11am–6pm, Sun noon–5pm // Age 5+

TIP: A hard day of spying calls for colorful French macarons, and the nearby Alliance Bakery offers a rainbow of these bright little bites with flavors drawn from the seasons.

107 _ WILLOWBROOK WILDLIFE CENTER

Caring for all creatures great and small

Chipmunks, cottontails, opossums, squirrels, songbirds, woodchucks, and woodpeckers – they too are residents of suburban Chicagoland. Willowbrook Wildlife Center is their go-to hospital, a place where all injured creatures, great and small, can count on receiving top-notch medical care as well as long-term rehabilitation. It's also a home for abandoned baby animals. The center cares for about 1,000 feathered and furry patients during the busy spring and summer months.

Though many critters are taken care of behind the scenes, over 90 species of injured, native, wild animals live here permanently, and you're welcome to say hello to them. This is a working animal hospital, so visitors can see the kitchen staff as they prepare special diets and even the nursery, where volunteers care for adorable baby bunnies, birds, and other tiny forest friends.

An outdoor hiking trail is lined with the new homes of animals with permanent disabilities, including eagles, hawks, turkey vultures, owls, red foxes, groundhogs, and raccoons. Take a kid-friendly hike along the half-mile outer loop and shorter inner loop, through 40 acres of restored prairie, savanna, woodland, and wetland habitats. A butterfly garden offers suggestions for trees and flowers that will make your own backyard into a haven for flutter-winged beauties.

If you find an injured wild animal in your own backyard, this is where you can find help (but check the center's wildlife rescue assessment and advice page at www.dupageforest.org/willowbrook-wildlife-center/wildlife-rescue and give a call before you hop in your animal ambulance).

TIP: Find all the plants you need to grow a butterfly haven in your own backyard at Farmers Market, Chicago's Garden Center.

Address 525 S. Park Boulevard, Glen Ellyn, IL 60137, +1 (630) 942-6200, www.dupageforest.org/willowbrook-wildlife-center // Getting there Metra UP-W to Glen Ellyn, then Pace bus 715 to Park & Falwell // Hours See website for hours // Ages 3+

108_ WINDY CITY ROLLERS

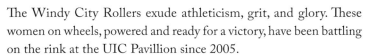

Got girl power?

The Windy City Rollers exude athleticism, grit, and glory. These women on wheels, powered and ready for a victory, have been battling on the rink at the UIC Pavillion since 2005.

With origins in the roller-skating marathons of the 1930s, roller derby is a contact sport played by two teams of five members roller-skating counterclockwise around a track in a series of short match-ups, a.k.a. jams. Both teams designate a jammer, whom you can easily identify by the star on their helmet. Her job is to score points by lapping members of the opposing team while her teammates attempt to hinder the opposing team's jammer.

The Windy City Rollers keep their jams kid-friendly; there are even a few moms-on-wheels among the team members. Kids will love the all-out excitement! They are sure to join in on the cheering and roaring from the many fans on hand to support our city's number one roller derby team. Though team members take plenty of hits and falls on the track, jams are built upon very strict rules enforced by referees, so this is no brawling free-for-all, but rather a safe zone for even little ones. It's fast, furious fun for the entire family.

Windy City has a four-team home league that includes teams with such incredible names as the Double Crossers, the Fury, Hell's Belles, and the Manic Attackers. These teams compete for an annual championship game named after Ivy King, the original superstar of roller derby. King started her derby skating career during the mid-1930s, when she traded her candy factory job for wheels.

Address UIC Pavilion, 525 S. Racine Avenue, Chicago, IL 60607, www.windycityrollers.com // Getting there Blue Line to UIC/Halsted // Hours See website for schedule // Ages 5+

TIP: Since you're on the UIC campus, take a minute to explore the Art & Architecture Building with its classic brutalist architectural style, crazy staircases, and oddly-shaped classrooms.

109_ WOOLLY MAMMOTH ANTIQUES

Bizarre bazaar

To enter Woolly Mammoth Antiques is to enter another dimension, where stuffed squirrels wear sombreros, shrunken heads and lanky skeletons still smile, and medical memorabilia of yesteryear – think uteri, kidney stones, and extracted molars preserved for eternity in formaldehyde – are showcased in all their gory glory. This is the only store in the city where you're bound to find an adorable pig fetus displayed next to a Victorian human hair wreath or a Brady Bunch lunchbox nestled below the light of a taxidermy alligator lamp. A wiener dog in a red velvet tuxedo serenades his sweetheart with a violin, and a two-headed turtle keeps watch.

If you're looking to amass your own cabinet of curiosities, you've come to the right place. This tiny, museum-like store is packed to the rafters with oddball items – vintage and antique taxidermy, skulls, bones, skeletons, funerary regalia, charts, maps, tools, specimens, natural history, science, culture, industry – that transport shoppers directly to the Twilight Zone.

Owner Adam Rust started collecting bones, teeth, and shells as a little boy, and he's usually on hand and happy to answer questions on the origin of each item. Almost everyone has been sourced by Rust himself. The inventory is constantly updated, so every visit here means you'll make plenty of discoveries as you browse the overflowing shelves. Prices range from $5 to the thousands.

Address 1513 W. Foster Avenue, Chicago, IL 60640, +1 (773) 989-3294, www.woollymammothchicago.com // Getting there Red Line to Berwyn // Hours Wed–Sun noon–7pm, Mon 1–7pm, Tue 3–7pm // Ages 3+

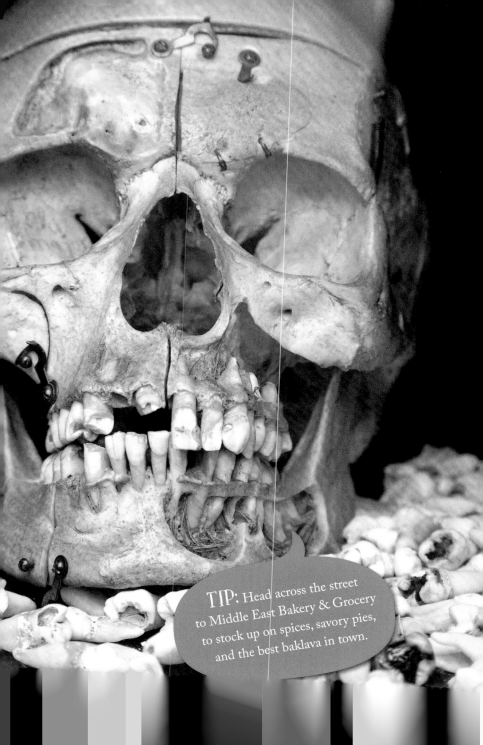

TIP: Head across the street to Middle East Bakery & Grocery to stock up on spices, savory pies, and the best baklava in town.

110_ WORLD'S LARGEST LAUNDROMAT

Making laundry fun since 1999

The World's Largest Laundromat has taken an annoying and time-consuming but necessary chore and turned it into – gasp – enjoyable family family entertainment time.

That's because the owner of this booming laundromat (boasting a 36-panel solar hot water system to boot) turned it into a space where you can wash and dry your duds and have a little fun, too.

Pile your clothes into one of over 300 machines, including massive 90-pound washers, and then enjoy the movie playing on one of the 16 flat-screen TVs suspended from the ceiling. A 90-inch-screen TV broadcasts all the big games and television events. Hang out with the birds at the avian exhibit. Play a video game in the arcade. A kids' play area with a Snoopy mobile keeps toddlers entertained. The homework area is a great space to solve those vexing arithmetic problems and review for the upcoming spelling bee together. Or bring a feast in from a nearby restaurant and settle in at one of the family-sized dining tables.

On Wednesdays and Sundays, live entertainment rolls out among the washers. Depending on the star, you can fold your clothes to the beat of a kindie rocker, get your face painted, count on a little homework help from a tutor, or put in a balloon animal request with the clown. Check the calendar and plan your laundry day accordingly.

The laundromat also hosts a summer reading program aptly named Read to Ride. For every book a 6- to-15-year-old reads over the summer, they can fill out a raffle ticket. At the end of the summer, the World's Largest Laundromat holds a big party to draw 20 winners.

Address 6246 W. Cermak Road, Berwyn, IL 60402, +1 (708) 749-1545, www.worldslargestlaundry.com // **Getting there** Pink Line to 54th/Cermak, then Pace bus 21 to Cermak/Lombard // **Hours** Open 24 hours // **Ages** 3+

TIP: Check out Play It Retro, a shop that sells, trades, and buys 'retro-current' video games.

111_ YAB HQ
You are beautiful

You are beautiful.

It's a phrase that every child – and adult – needs to take to heart.

In Chicago, these simple yet meaningful words popped up across the city starting in 2002, when artist Matthew Hoffman printed the message on 100 stickers, reminding everyone that we all have value and that we all have something special to bring forth in this world. Three million stickers and several art installations later, Hoffman's words have provided encouragement beyond his wildest dreams.

At the You Are Beautiful Headquarters, a.k.a. YAB HQ, you can go behind the scenes and see how Hoffman and his team are working to spread positivity far and wide across our city. Browse the gallery and take home a reminder of just how special you are. Stickers, woodcuts, T-shirts, and notebooks all feature Hoffman's simple, inspiring graphic messages. *You are Beautiful. Take Care of Others and Let Others Take Care of You. It's Okay to Not Be Okay. Anything is Possible. Go for It.* Alternatively, take part in one of the HQ's many uplifting, family-friendly workshops which include yoga, healthy cooking, the opportunity to customize your own woodcut, studio tours, T-shirt making, and more.

"I know the times where I have been uplifted by something either simple or funny and interesting," Hoffman told the *Chicago Tribune* in 2015. "Those little moments can make a big difference, even though it might not feel like it at the time. I just wanted to add to that and be part of that conversation."

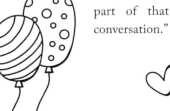

TIP: It's hard to miss the 11-foot x 15-foot You Are Beautiful "sticker" weighing in at around 1,000 lbs. that stands just off the Oakwood Exit of South Lake Shore Drive.

Address 3368 N. Elston Avenue, Chicago, IL 60618, +1 (312) 623-8249, www.you-are-beautiful.com, hi@you-are-beautiful.com // **Getting there** Blue Line to Belmont or Addison // **Hours** Daily 11am–7pm // Ages 5+

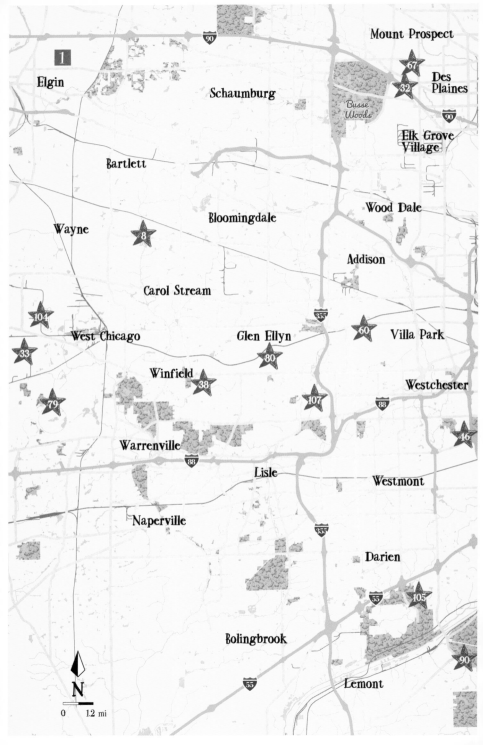

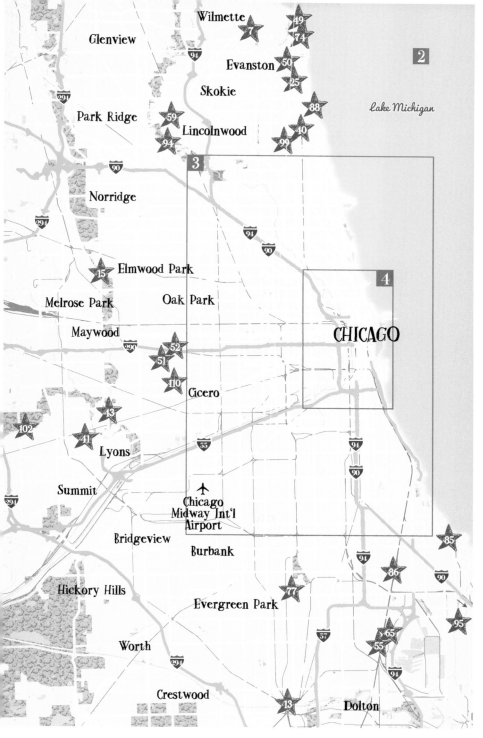

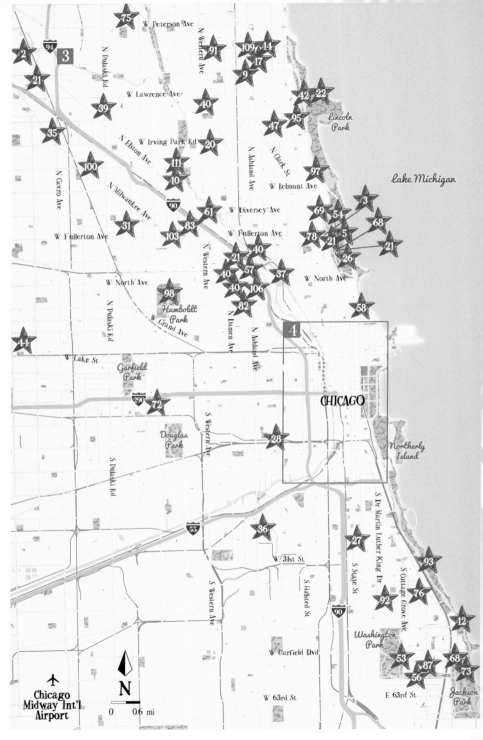

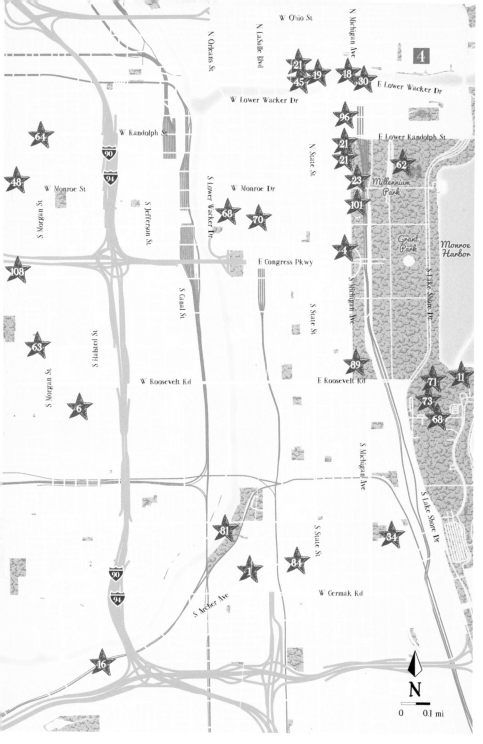

Amy Bizzarri, Susie Inverso
111 Places in Chicago
That You Must Not Miss
ISBN 978-3-7408-0156-4

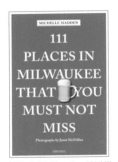

Michelle Madden, Janet McMillan
111 Places in Milwaukee
That You Must Not Miss
ISBN 978-3-7408-0491-6

Dave Doroghy, Graeme Menzies
111 Places in Vancouver
That You Must Not Miss
ISBN 978-3-7408-0494-7

Kevin C. Fitzpatrick, Joe Conzo
111 Places in the Bronx
That You Must Not Miss
ISBN 978-3-7408-0492-3

Floriana Petersen, Steve Werney
111 Places in Silicon Valley
That You Must Not Miss
ISBN 978-3-7408-0493-0

Leslie Adatto, Clay Williams
111 Rooftops in New York
That You Must Not Miss
ISBN 978-3-7408-0495-4

John Major, Ed Lefkowicz
111 Places in Brooklyn
That You Must Not Miss
ISBN 978-3-7408-0380-3

Wendy Lubovich, Ed Lefkowicz
111 Museums in New York
That You Must Not Miss
ISBN 978-3-7408-0379-7

Anita Mai Genua, Clare Davenport,
Elizabeth Lenell Davies
111 Places in Toronto
That You Must Not Miss
ISBN 978-3-7408-0257-8

Andréa Seiger, John Dean
111 Places in Washington D.C.
That You Must Not Miss
ISBN 978-3-7408-0258-5

Elisabeth Larsen
111 Places in The Twin Cities
That You Must Not Miss
ISBN 978-3-7408-0029-1

Joe DiStefano, Clay Williams
111 Places in Queens
That You Must Not Miss
ISBN 978-3-7408-0020-8

Allison Robicelli, John Dean
111 Places in Baltimore
That You Must Not Miss
ISBN 978-3-7408-0158-8

Laurel Moglen, Julia Posey,
Lyudmila Zotova
111 Places in Los Angeles
That You Must Not Miss
ISBN 978-3-95451-884-5

Floriana Petersen,
Steve Werney
111 Places in San Francisco
That You Must Not Miss
ISBN 978-3-95451-609-4

Jo-Anne Elikann
111 Places in New York
That You Must Not Miss
ISBN 978-3-95451-052-8

Michael Murphy, Sally Asher
111 Places in New Orleans
That You Must Not Miss
ISBN 978-3-95451-645-2

Gordon Streisand
111 Places in Miami
and the Keys
That You Must Not Miss
ISBN 978-3-95451-644-5

Laszlo Trankovits
111 Places in Jerusalem
That You Shouldn't Miss
ISBN 978-3-7408-0320-9

Beate C. Kirchner
111 Places in Rio de Janeiro
That You Must Not Miss
ISBN 978-3-7408-0262-2

Benjamin Haas, Leonie Friedrich
111 Places in Buenos Aires
That You Must Not Miss
ISBN 978-3-7408-0260-8

John Sykes, Birgit Weber
111 Places in London
That You Shouldn't Miss
ISBN 978-3-95451-346-8

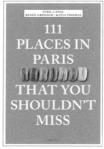

Sybil Canac, Renée Grimaud,
Katia Thomas
111 Places in Paris
That You Shouldn't Miss
ISBN 978-3-7408-0159-5

Kai Oidtmann
111 Places in Iceland
That You Shouldn't Miss
ISBN 978-3-7408-0030-7

Gillian Tait
111 Places in Edinburgh
That You Shouldn't Miss
ISBN 978-3-95451-883-8

Alexia Amvrazi, Diana Farr
Louis, Diane Shugart,
Yannis Varouhakis
111 Places in Athens
That You Shouldn't Miss
ISBN 978-3-7408-0377-3

Christoph Hein, Sabine Hein
111 Places in Singapore
That You Shouldn't Miss
ISBN 978-3-7408-0382-7

Acknowledgments

Thank you to Justin, my husband and assistant, for visiting so many wonderful places with me not only to make this book, but in regular life, too. Thank you to my friends who let me 'borrow' their kids for the book: Airan, Tom, Bree, and Emily. And thank you to all my friends and family for their love and encouragement.   S.I.

Authors

Amy Bizzarri is a freelance travel writer focused on family, food, and fun, with a special interest in family adventure travel. A teacher with 20+ years of experience and a Master of Arts in Education with a focus on bilingual education, Amy believes that learning is best accompanied by a big dose of fun. When she isn't writing, you'll find her on her bicycle, exploring her beloved hometown city of Chicago with her two children.

Susie Inverso has spent many years running around Chicago photographing the CTA public transit system, and photographs weddings and portraits for her company, Crimson Cat Studios. When she's not photographing trains, people, or pets, she plays the trumpet and guitar in various musical projects, and enjoys road trips with her husband, Justin. They live on the North Side with their two cats and box turtle.